AN ESSAY ON METHOD

AN *ESSAY* ON

Method

by

C. HILLIS KAISER

Rutgers University Press

NEW BRUNSWICK   NEW JERSEY

1952

CONTENTS

AN ESSAY ON METHOD

[ONE]

The Fundamental Problem

1. *THE DIVISIONS IN CONTEMPORARY CULTURE*

OUR contemporary society seems to be unique in at least one respect. Never before has there been such a wide diffusion of the traditional cultural forces and never before such a disunity among these forces themselves. Today, thanks to our system of education, every citizen can read, write, and do simple sums. He has read HAMLET, has heard of Plato and Michelangelo, and admires the achievements of Mr. Einstein. There is no sharp line dividing the cultured classes of our society from the uncultured. Instead there is a continuous spectrum which extends from the uneducated few at the one end to the cultural elite at the other. Culture is no longer the possession of an exclusive fraternity of "doctors"; it lies within the reach and means of all.

The result is that there are no longer horizontal stratifications in our contemporary world such as characterized previous epochs. The stratifications or divisions are now vertical rather than horizontal. The lines are drawn between those educated, well or badly, in one cultural activity and those educated in another, between the scientists and the philosophers, the artists and the theologians. This too has been produced by education, in particular by the specialized education we give our youth in our colleges and universities. It is true that lip service is paid to what are called "general

3

education requirements," but usually all sense of the reason for such requirements has disappeared. The student is merely assured that he will be a better engineer if he knows a little (but not too much) philosophy, a better artist if he knows a little science, a better psychologist if he knows a little literature. The result is that if a student has been badly educated in his chosen field he knows nothing when he graduates, and if he has been well educated, he knows merely his own field and nothing of other fields or of their relation to his own.

This type of education has been carried on for over a generation in America and is being imitated in France and England, with the result that the divisions in contemporary culture are now becoming obvious. It is common knowledge that poetry is no longer written for the educated world; it is written for other poets. Serious science, of course, is written for no one but the specialist, or if it is a popular book, it is written with such condescension that the author would appear to be addressing an audience of children. Philosophers, with one or two exceptions, are a completely ineffective force in American culture, principally because their jargon is intelligible only to other philosophers. Plato, Descartes, Berkeley, and Hume, to mention no others, wrote philosophy in the "vulgar tongue" without renouncing either seriousness or precision.

The result is that anyone who submits to the education prevalent in our society must renounce the hope of seeing life steadily and seeing it whole. He is forced to look at the world and the other disciplines from the perspective of his own. Such perspectives are usually arbitrary and preposterous, and their preposterousness is most in evidence when scientists write about religion or theologians about science. The members of one of these vertical strata not merely have no knowledge of the ideas or methods common to another stratum; they cannot understand how anyone can *be* a member of another stratum. Ignorance in this case breeds not merely misunderstanding but intolerance.

2. *THE BOUNDARIES OF THE FUNDAMENTAL DISCIPLINES*

W H A T the inhabitant of an isolated stratum seems to require is a map [1] of certain fundamental disciplines, such as science, art, philosophy, and religion, with an indication of the relation of his discipline to other disciplines and a statement of the advantages to be derived from pursuing each of them. Such a statement will implicitly inform him of the limitations of his own discipline, silence his cultural intolerance and belligerence, and broaden his cultural sympathies. It is the intent of this essay to provide such a map.

The difficulties in the way of constructing a map of this sort are obvious. First of all, it must be intelligible to the members of every discipline in the same sense that a good map of Europe must be intelligible to the inhabitants of each constituent country. In discussing the nature of any one discipline one must therefore forego the use of the technical jargon peculiar to that discipline and use instead a neutral language, that of ordinary educated speech. One must construct an account of each discipline in this neutral language which will not offend the specialists in the field and yet be intelligible to the members of other disciplines.

Secondly, one must be quite sure that in such a map there is no overlapping. There must be no disputed territories. The relation between one discipline and another is hardly clarified by the statement that in certain instances the two are fused. Confusion is engendered on this point by the fact that a single *object* can be the product of two or more diverse

[1] I have borrowed this term from R. G. Collingwood. Cf. his *Speculum Mentis*, Oxford, 1924.

activities. Thus a piece of religious music is the outcome of a
genuine religious experience and is simultaneously a work
of art, but what makes it religious is quite different from
what makes it artistic. What is needed is a set of distinctions,
in the same sense that one requires sharply defined boundaries in a geographical map. One wishes to know where
science leaves off and philosophy begins, where philosophy
leaves off and religion begins, and so on.

3. *THE FUNDAMENTAL PROBLEM OF*
   METHODOLOGY

To give an account of a discipline it is enough to give a
precise statement of how that discipline is carried on. One
gives an account of science, for instance, when one describes
how scientists behave when they are functioning as scientists.
One knows what art is when one knows how it is done, and
not until then, and we can say the same of philosophy,
technology, and religion. But to know how science is done is
to know the methods which are characteristic of science, and
therefore to give an account of a discipline is to give an
account of the methods characteristic of that discipline. We
are accustomed to the phrase "scientific method," but according to this point of view, there is likewise philosophic
method, artistic method, and religious method. (I shall
assume throughout the early phases of this discussion that
there are only four fundamental disciplines—art, science,
philosophy, and religion, and defer until the final chapter
any discussion of the evidence for this important assumption.)

Our initial problem was to give an account of the fundamental disciplines and their relations to one another. We
can now say that our problem is to give an account of the
methods of art, science, philosophy, and religion and of the

relations of these methods to one another. It is convenient to call the enterprise which attempts to determine the methods of these disciplines simply "methodology," and we shall regard it, until evidence to the contrary turns up, as an independent discipline which is not identical with any of the fundamental disciplines. We shall assume, for example, that the activity of determining the methods of science is not itself scientific and the activity of determining the methods of religion is not religious.

We are forced by this assumption, however, to "give an account" of methodology itself, and this means, as we have seen, that we must give an account of how methodology is to be carried on. To put it briefly, if somewhat tortuously, we wish to know "the proper method of methodology," that is, we wish to know how we ought to go about determining the methods of the fundamental disciplines. There are clearly alternative modes of procedure, and we would like to find the best one, the one we *ought* to follow. Our problem can be phrased this way because we know in advance the end at which methodology aims, and this we do not know in the case of the basic disciplines. In fact it is the function of methodology to tell us finally what the ends of each of these disciplines are. When we ask for the proper way to do methodology we are asking for an account of that procedure which will enable us to determine the methods of the fundamental disciplines and their relations to each other. To "justify" any proposed procedure of this sort is merely to demonstrate that if we adopt it we shall be able to do what we want to do.

Historically considered, there are two principal kinds of methodology. We shall call them "objective methodology" and "polemic methodology." Objective methodology attempts as honestly as possible to determine what the methods of the fundamental disciplines are and how they are related to each other. Polemic methodology attempts to show that the methods of some disciplines are "better" than the methods of others. Thus it might be said that the method of experiment is better than the method of intuition or the method of authority. Such a statement is meaningless, however, unless we are told *in what respects* experiment is better than the other methods. If what is meant is that experiment is a better method for determining empirical fact than intuition or authority, then no one will dispute this proposition. It could be argued with equal persuasiveness that if one wishes to do metaphysics, then intuition is better than experiment. Likewise experiment is useless for religious purposes and could better be replaced by the method of authority. If the experimentalist intends to assert that it is better to pursue experimental fact rather than religious or metaphysical insight, then this is something which he cannot demonstrate by experiment; it is simply a statement of personal preference. Thus the polemic methodologist asserts either the trivial proposition that it is better to use a certain method when one is interested in results obtainable only by that method, or he asserts the indemonstrable proposition that it is better in some absolute sense to pursue one discipline rather than another. There is no proof that it is better to be a mathematician than a saint or better to be a saint than a mathematician. Science and religion ought to be regarded as complementary components in the single ideal of human perfection. It is the business of objective methodology to tell us what the method of each of these disciplines is. Once the method has been determined, it is the business of education to determine the contribution which each discipline makes to the single ideal of human perfection.

4. *METHODOLOGY AND DEFINITION*

O u r fundamental problem, we said, was to discover a procedure which would enable us to determine the nature and relations of the fundamental disciplines, and we re-phrased this by saying that we wished to determine the methods of each discipline and the relations of these methods to one another. But we could also say that we know the nature of a given discipline only when we have a definition of the word used to denote that discipline. It is this sort of explicit knowledge which we require in methodology. The end of methodology according to this view is the construction of definitions of such words as "art," "science," "philoso-phy," and "religion." The problem of justifying the proce-dure of methodology becomes the problem of justifying our procedure in constructing these definitions.

Such definitions cannot be wholly arbitrary, that is, they cannot be "stipulated" or "nominal" definitions of the sort one makes up in mathematics and the other sciences. They must be "real" definitions in the sense that they conform, as best they can, to the actual facts of common usage. There is no "real" meaning in any other sense to which our definitions must conform. We must admit that there is literally no universal agreement concerning the usage of such words as "science" and "art," but this need not prevent us from respecting agreement when it actually does exist. We may all disagree concerning the exact usage of the word "art," but we agree nevertheless that some Shakespearean sonnets and some Mozart quartets should be called "works of art" rather than something else. It is this common core of agreement to which our real definitions must conform, and it is this sort of agreement which we shall mean when we refer hereafter to "common" or "ordinary" usage.

According to this view when we assert that "man is a rational animal" is a real definition of "man," we are saying that it is customary for all (or most) users of the word "man" to agree that it can be replaced wherever it occurs by the expression "rational animal," and conversely that "rational animal" can always be replaced by "man." Our assertion may be false, of course, if these expressions are not actually used interchangeably. Let us suppose that we had recommended the alternative definition, "Man is a living being that possesses the power of reasoning." The linguistic form of this definition is different from that of the first, but presumably all individuals that are called "men" according to the first would be called "men" according to the second and conversely. Whenever this does occur, let us say that our definitions have the same "content" but a different "form." It is then obvious that the exact form of the definition is something over which we have some control, but the content is fixed by usage.

Since we have this freedom of disposition with respect to the form of our definitions, we can now state exactly the procedure we must follow in defining the words which are to denote our fundamental disciplines. The content of each definition must conform to what we have called "common usage," but we can choose that form of definition which best reveals the relationships that exist between the disciplines. By this procedure we can take account of those two conditions which we agreed must be respected in constructing adequate accounts of our disciplines: that our procedure will enable us to give an account (1) of the nature of each discipline and (2) of the relations which hold between the fundamental disciplines. This general mode of constructing definitions I shall call "the procedure of coördination."

The objection may be raised that we can say nothing about the relations of our disciplines until we know everything about each of them. This contention is patently false, however, as a little reflection will show. One of the most general questions which we could ask about our disciplines is: Do the words "science," "art," "philosophy," and "religion" ordinarily denote actions or do they denote objects? Do they denote activities or products of activities? We talk of art-objects, of philosophical and religious writings, of scientific treatises, but we also talk of philosophizing, of religious practices, of composing and painting and writing. There is literally no universal agreement here, but, as we shall see, our conception of the relation between these disciplines is much clearer if we agree to respect that usage which considers each of our disciplines as an activity. Art-objects, philosophic treatises, religious paraphernalia can then be regarded as the products or instruments of such activities. What is important is that we need not know *in detail* what sort of activity art is in order to agree that it is an activity, and this holds true for the other disciplines.

If we agree that each of our disciplines is an activity, we can ask of each: Is it a purely human activity or is it an activity which we share with other animals? The answer must be provided by common usage, but if the answer to this question is affirmative for each discipline (and I shall argue in Chapter Two that it is), we then know at this stage of our analysis that each discipline is a purely human activity. We can now proceed to ask of each discipline: Is it an activity of making something or is it some other sort of human activity? If it is an activity of making, we can ask: What kinds of things does it make or what kind of making is it? If it is not an activity of making something but an activity of discovering something, we can then ask: What kinds of things does it discover? or more generally, What kind of discovery activity is it? By a continuation of this systematic questioning we shall finally arrive at certain answers which are the exact definitions we are looking for, and by reason of the way in which these definitions have been constructed they should declare at once how each of our disciplines is related to each of the others.

5. *DEFINITIONS AND INSTANCES*

THE method of definition we have recommended follows closely Plato's celebrated method of division. In the PHAE-DRUS [2] Plato suggests that there are two steps in the construction of any adequate definition. The first is "that of perceiving and bringing together in one idea the scattered particulars, that one may make clear by definition the particular thing which he wishes to explain." The word "idea" here is to be taken in the sense of "class," and this first step corresponds to our observation that all our disciplines are activities and in fact purely human activities. This first step Plato would call "making a collection." The second step is "that of dividing things again by classes, where the natural joints are, and not trying to break any part, after the manner of a bad carver." This corresponds to our division of human activities into those which are activities of making something and those which are not. This second step is repeated until we have a clear-cut definition of each of our disciplines. Plato's warning that we must always divide "where the natural joints are" corresponds to our principle that common usage must always be respected.

The method of division enables us to "corner" a specific class of activities which we propose to call "art," another class which we call "science," and so on. Our definitions are always definitions of *kinds* of activities. In practice, however, we are always concerned with particular activities. If we ask, "Is this design a work of art?" we are asking, "Should the activity of making this design be classified as an artistic activity?" We may rephrase this simply, "Is the activity of making this design an instance of art?" Clearly our definitions must enable us to answer questions of this sort, if they are to be of any practical use. It would be an additional

[2] 265 D-E., tr. by H. N. Fowler, Loeb Classical Library, Heinemann, 1926.

advantage if they provided answers to hypothetical questions of the sort Joyce propounds: [3] "If a man, hacking in fury at a block of wood, make there an image of a cow, is this a work of art? If not, why not?" Joyce is propounding two questions here, rather than one, but an "ideal" definition of "art" would enable us to answer both of them.

We have agreed that our definitions, as far as possible, should respect the canons of common usage, and we can express this condition by saying that whatever is considered to be art by common usage must be an instance of art according to our definition. Thus any definition of art from which it would follow that no Shakespearean tragedy is a work of art would be inadequate, since it is universally held that some (if not all) Shakespearean tragedies are works of art. In particular, a theory of art which held that all art is merely imitative representation of objects or emotions would be inadequate since it would exclude "The Well-tempered Clavichord" and Chartres cathedral, and these are universally regarded as works of art.

It does not follow, however, that what is an instance of art according to our definition must be acknowledged as art by common usage, since we have seen that an ideal definition must provide unambiguous answers even in those cases where there is no common agreement. Our definition, for example, must enable us to decide whether cooking is or is not an instance of art, even if common agreement is lacking, and likewise we ought to be able to answer hypothetical questions of the sort Joyce propounds which are framed to defy any appeal to common usage. Our definitions therefore will be broader than those provided by an analysis of usage, but they will not conflict with usage; they will simply provide clear-cut answers in those cases where usage is non-commit-

[3] James Joyce, *A Portrait of the Artist as a Young Man*, Modern Library, 1928, p. 251.

tal. The important cases concern those activities which lie on the borderline between two fundamental disciplines where common agreement is notoriously non-existent. Our ideal definitions must tell us explicitly how such activities should be classified. This is equivalent to saying that our definitions must establish the exact boundaries between our fundamental disciplines — boundaries, moreover, which dare not overlap. If our definitions have been properly constructed, they will provide us with a map of our four disciplines which will be consistent with ordinary usage and in which the boundaries of each discipline and its relations to the others will be clearly defined. This, as we have seen, is the proper goal of methodology.

6. ALTERNATIVE PROCEDURES

T H E traditional view is that methodology is a branch of philosophy. This position is supported by the fact that we speak of "the philosophy of art," "the philosophy of science," "the philosophy of religion" when we refer to inquiries concerning the methods of these disciplines. According to this view, a general name for methodology would be simply "philosophy of ——." The defenders of this view are ready to point out that many, if not most, of the important contributions to methodology have been made by philosophers, but this in itself is hardly a convincing argument, since many of the great philosophers have also been scientists and yet we never propose to call their science "philosophy." We must consider the question on its own merits and ask ourselves whether we seriously propose to use the methods of philosophy in methodology.

If it is the business of methodology to determine the methods of the fundamental disciplines and if philosophy is itself one of the fundamental disciplines, then we are proposing to use the methods of philosophy to determine the methods of philosophy. But this is clearly absurd. Either we know at the beginning of such an inquiry what the methods of philosophy are or we do not know. If we do not know, then it is highly improbable, if not impossible, that we shall use them in the inquiry. If we do know, then we are committed to finding out what we already know, and an impartial observer might ask us how we know initially what philosophy is. If philosophy is one of the fundamental disciplines, then according to the traditional view there ought to be a "philosophy of philosophy," but we never use this expression. It would reveal too clearly the absurdity of the traditional procedure.

The fact is that philosophers are apt to be critical of everything except the propriety of their own procedures. A truly objective methodology must attempt to determine the proper methods of philosophy, as well as those of science, art, and religion, and it can do this only by getting outside each of these disciplines. Any attempt to use the methods of philosophy or science or religion or art in methodology itself can lead only to an untenable circularity and dogmatism. In this respect the procedure of coördination is clearly preferable to any form of the traditional procedure.

Our procedure of coördination will be criticized from another point of view by the partisans of a descriptive or empirical procedure in methodology. According to these methodologists, if we want to find out what science is, we ought to study the behavior of scientists and the products of their activities; our first step is to isolate scientific activities from all other activities and then by patient study and analysis find out what the actual methods of science are. Let us call this "the procedure of isolation." The proponent of this procedure will insist that our comparative method is cumbersome and dogmatic and that it does not conform to the facts.

Our own reply must be, "But how do you know which activities are scientific?" If the "isolationist" knows in all cases how to tell a scientific activity from a non-scientific, he already knows what science is. If he does not know, then he cannot apply his own procedure. Shall we include alchemy and astrology among the scientific activities we propose to isolate and study? If we can answer such questions, then we must have initially a fairly clear conception of science. We must know at any rate how it can be distinguished from technology and magic. But how do we get this "knowledge"?

The procedure of isolation is indispensable in all those areas where there is universal agreement concerning the meaning of the fundamental terms, and our own procedure of coördination will make restricted use of it. It fails, however, for all those borderline cases where there is no common agreement. An ideal set of definitions on the other hand should enable us to classify each of these activities without violating the canons of common usage. Such a set of definitions should enable us to construct a map of our four disciplines in which there will be no fuzzy boundaries, no disputed territories, and no overlapping. Our procedure of coördination promises to provide us with such a map, and this cannot be said of the procedure of isolation.

With this brief exposition and defense of our coördinate procedure we can now proceed to put it to actual use in elaborating the fundamental distinctions between our four disciplines.

[TWO]

The Primary Distinctions

1. *ACTIVITIES AND PRODUCTS OF ACTIVITIES*

W E have assumed in our preceding discussion that the terms we intend to define designate classes of activities. This requires some defence, since it is often asserted that science is a collection of statements of fact or of arguments, that art is a collection of art-objects, and religion a body of doctrines and codes. It is important to recognize that objects or things do not constitute the primary phenomena or elements of each discipline but are rather the products or records of actions which do constitute these elements. The classical scholar is forced by his method to identify a man's philosophy with his writings, since no other evidence is available, but if this identification were generally accepted, then Socrates, who wrote no philosophy, would not be a philosopher. Plato reminds us in the PHAEDRUS [1] that even in the case of those philosophers who do write, the writing is never adequate to the thinking. It is at best an imperfect record of the thinking. The same can be said of any spoken sentences. They are merely evidence that philosophizing is or was going on. What is important is to realize that philosophizing can go on without spoken or written utterance. For this reason Plato defines thinking in the THEAETETUS [2] as

[1] 276 C.
[2] 189 E.

the mind's conversation with itself. The same distinction is even more obvious in science where the experimenter is faced with the difficulty of writing up his experiment. Unless the experimenter is a consummate literary craftsman, it is often impossible to tell from the write-up exactly what was done, and yet *this*, not the write-up, is the scientific achievement.

The confusion of art with "art-objects" is perhaps more general and is fostered by a preoccupation with literary and visual art. In the case of those arts which depend on performance there is no object which can be preserved in a museum or library, although the directions for performance — the scores and scripts — can be so preserved. In the case of the dance the absence of a specific "art-object" is rather more obvious by reason of the lack of an adequate notation. In the case of all impromptu performances there is no pre-existent set of directions and no bar therefore to the identification of the art-object with the performance itself. A "work of art," considered as an object, is merely a record or product of artistic activity, and it is this activity which is an instance of art, not its products.

Similar remarks apply in the case of religion. We are apt to identify a religion with a set of doctrines or rules of conduct. Doctrines by themselves, however, are merely the inert record of vanished religious vision or an enticement to the act of belief and commitment. They are nothing without belief, and belief is an action of the will. In the same way codes of conduct are bare formulae unless they are acted upon. The anthropologist knows this clearly and seeks the religion of a group in its actual practices. The fact is that religion in all of its phases, whether public ritual or private worship or mystical contemplation, is a matter of practice, and it is simple carelessness to confuse practice with the records or apparatus of practice. Common sense is clear on this point and defines hypocrisy as a discrepancy between what a man professes to believe and what he does. White-head's definition of religion as "what a man *does* with his own solitariness" [3] (italics mine) simply corroborates this insight.

There is another error which appears when we attempt to identify a discipline with a certain set of objects. Because an object is one and unique, we tend to assume that it must belong to one and only one discipline. The phrase "work of art" suggests that certain things are *merely* works of art and nothing else. But every art-object is more than a work of art, as every art dealer knows. It is also an economic object, a physical object, a chemical object. It may even be the record of a religious experience or an attempt to portray concretely some subtle philosophic insight. Lucretius' great poem belongs to science and philosophy as well as to litera-ture. A great novel can be more than a work of art, and it can be great therefore in two senses: first, because of its excellence as a work of art, and secondly, because it is *more* than a work of art. It is a simple confusion of categories when we praise a literary artist for his knowledge of human nature or his learning or the accuracy of his descriptions. This is praising his scientific achievements, not his artistic. The commonest vice of literary criticism is to praise the author and not the artist.

We must not attempt to classify *objects* therefore in our efforts to distinguish our fundamental disciplines. We must learn instead to distinguish in each object that which makes it a scientific object, that which makes it philosophic, and so on, remembering that what makes it scientific is not identical with that which makes it philosophic or artistic or religious. We must attempt to define our primitive terms without assuming that instances of pure art or pure science or pure philosophy ever do occur. Even when we attend to activities

[3] A. N. Whitehead, *Religion in the Making*, Macmillan, 1926, p. 16.

rather than to objects we must remember that pure scientific activity or pure artistic activity may never occur. It is nevertheless by virtue of approximation to the ideal expressed in our definitions that we shall call certain activities "artistic" and certain objects "works of art."

2. *HUMAN AND NON-HUMAN*

OUR primary class or genus therefore is a class of activities, but we must not thoughtlessly presuppose that these must be human activities. We may arbitrarily divide activities into "human" and "non-human," but we must look to common usage to provide an answer to the question, "Are the fundamental disciplines solely human activities?"

No one, to my knowledge, has seriously suggested that any animal other than man is religious nor that animals philosophize. Plato, it is true, compares the philosopher and the dog [4] but in the same sense presumably that he compares the sophist to a wolf. Pythagoras, too, stopped a man from beating a dog because he recognized in its howls the voice of a dead friend, presumably a philosopher. These are hardly instances of *common* usage, however, and our question, if applied only to religion and philosophy, would ordinarily be regarded as absurd.

It is quite otherwise with respect to science and art. Certain constructive activities of ants or spiders or birds are often described by naturalists in such a way that it is difficult not to call them "scientific." The spider, the lark, the nightingale might equally well be called artists and have been so called by many a poet. According to Fabre,[5] the great French naturalist, a certain species of spider constructs a web which is almost a perfect logarithmic spiral and operates

[4] 376 A.

[5] J. H. Fabre, *The Life of the Spider*, tr. by A. T. de Mattos, Dodd Mead, 1915, pp. 383–400.

with an uncanny "knowledge" of the laws of statics. The mysterious knowledge possessed by the spider of the cervical vertebrae of the victim it intends to paralyze is equally impressive.

But clearly we must distinguish between what is scientific in the *account* and what is scientific in the *activity* itself. It is clearly the naturalist who knows about logarithmic spirals and cervical vertebrae. What is mysterious in the activity of the spider is that it acts *without* knowing. This is revealed, as a matter of fact, in certain crises. Fabre observed in the case of a certain female spider that when the time came for her to spin a sac for her eggs she was quite willing to spin it with equally elaborate care about some cork pellets provided as a substitute. Of such organisms one can say merely that they act as if they were little machines constructed by a scientist. Pappus, the great Alexandrian geometer, in praising the sagacity of bees in choosing the hexagon as the side of the cells in their honeycombs, said: "Bees, then, know just this fact which is of service to themselves, that the hexagon is greater than the square and the triangle and will hold more honey for the same expenditure of material used in constructing the different figures." [6] But he needed to admit that this "geometrical forethought" was not a product of reason but of a "certain natural instinct" given them by God.

Nor is there any reason to assert that the nightingale is an artist because of the beauty of her song. One might conceivably find colors on certain flowers that are more pleasing than those in many paintings, yet one would not conclude that the flower is an artist because it produces this lovely color. A human singer who produced only one song on every occasion would finally, by reason of this limitation in repertoire, be treated like a music box. The nightingale as artist is

[6] M. R. Cohen and I. E. Drabkin, *A Source Book in Greek Science*, McGraw-Hill, 1948, p. 81.

a theme for poetry just as the spider as scientist is a theme for science. Neither comparison is to be taken seriously.

The root of this confusion, if any remains in the popular mind, is this: that skill is identified with science and craft is identified with art, or both science and art are considered as forms of craft (*technē*). If it can be shown, and this I propose to do in the course of the discussion, that neither science nor art is a kind of craft, then most of the temptation to call non-human activities "scientific" or "artistic" will be removed.

3. *PLAYFUL AND SERIOUS*

LET us now separate off those activities which are done for the sake of the characteristic pleasure which accompanies the activity itself, and let us call all such activities "play." We are reminded that there are such activities by the expressions "child's play," "playing a game," "playing an instrument," "the play," and so on. Our class contains activities, however, that are not usually called "play." The activity of a gourmet, if he is sincere and not histrionic, is a case of play in our sense. Any operation, from the meanest drudgery to the most adventurous schemes of global strategy, can become play if it is done for the sake of the thrill or satisfaction one obtains in doing it.

We can now attempt to determine whether each of our disciplines is or is not a kind of play. Plato's answer concerning art was unequivocal: imitative art, he said in the REPUBLIC [7] and SOPHIST, [8] is a kind of play, a kind of play which makes images. This account of art as a species of play has been repeated by many modern aestheticians. The layman's conviction that the artist is mad or, if an "old master,"

[7] 602 B.
[8] 235 A–236 C.

inspired, springs from a confused recognition that art is created from a curious inner necessity, without physical compulsion, inducement, or reward. It is this which puzzles and intrigues the practical man. He usually concludes that the artist was aiming at fame and that he finally got what he was after, but he is forced to admit that the living artists he knows seem not to desire anything beyond the opportunity to pursue their accomplishment. They are wild, impractical creatures who must be treated indulgently like children or idiots.

The academic mind is equally confused. Learned, bookish people are convinced that the artist must be as serious as they are: he is in their eyes a superscientist or a metaphysician, ready to reveal to us the inmost secrets of nature if we would only listen; he is a psychologist who probes into the deepest recesses of the human soul; he is a remorseless analyst and reformer who exposes the ills and fevers of society; he is a physician who purges our passions with honeyed cathartics. To serious and practical people the artist is a mystery, with the result that he is either laughed at or deified according to the measure of his success. Children, however, and certain "primitive" peoples, do not need to have the *purpose* of art explained to them. They have at once an immediate and natural sympathy with the intent of the artist. What they cannot understand is why anyone should prefer to be serious rather than playful.

This opposition of "playful" and "serious" needs to be clarified, however. If to be "serious" means to be "wholly absorbed in the task at hand" or "completely aware of its intrinsic importance," then the child at play is more serious than the adult at work. This is not the sense in which I propose to use the word. We must recur, in fact, to our implicit division of activities into the playful and the nonplayful. The latter will consist of all those activities which are done for the sake of something other than the characteristic pleasure which accompanies them. They may be done by reason of physical compulsion or for material gain or for discipline of the will or for spiritual elevation; the end aimed at lies outside the activity itself and beyond the pleasure which accompanies the activity. They are done, in short, for the sake of an *outcome* considered important or beneficial or to avoid an outcome considered trivial or harmful. It would be tempting to call all these activities "work" were it not for the paradox that, by reason of our Puritan heritage or our economic philosophy, work has been given an intrinsic dignity of its own. What is common to all such activities is that they are not done for the sake of the pleasure (if any) which accompanies the doing of them.

It is equally impossible to label all such activities "serious," since it would then follow that the antics of circus clowns and newspaper columnists were serious. We usually reserve the word "serious" for those activities of which the outcome has an immediate bearing on the well-being of the agent or, more generally, on the well-being of those individuals affected by the activity. Thus the decisions of prime ministers or of business executives are serious in this sense, but the penitential ritual of the saint in his cloister is no less serious. Seriousness, in other words, is not a matter of numbers. An action is serious if it is done for the sake of assuring the well-being of *someone*, and this "someone" may be merely the individual agent himself.

4. ART AND SCIENCE AS PLAYFUL

IT is unfortunate that Plato, who first expressed the insight that "art is a kind of play and nothing serious," should not have observed that the same is true of science. Plato, however, was a Pythagorean, and science was for him merely a means of purifiying or "saving" the soul. The fundamental idea of Platonic ethics is that virtue is a kind of harmony in the soul which is best attained by the mind disciplined to perceive the harmonies and beauties in mathematics and astronomy. It is undeniable that science has an important educational function, and the emphasis on this function we owe to Plato, but it does not follow that the definition of science must include a reference to this function. If we attend to the nature of science and not its possible uses, clearly it is a form of play, as we are using the word. It is an activity done for the sake of the peculiar joy of *discovery*.

We are so accustomed to consider merely the uses of science, whether as an educational tool or a means to the control of nature, and so apt therefore to confuse science and technology, that we find it difficult to admit that science, as well as art, is playful. Pythagoras and his followers pursued science for the sake of purifying the soul, Francis Bacon and his successors for the sake of controlling nature, and our conceptions of science have been largely determined by these two schools. For either school science is unquestionably serious and can be justified only by its fruits.

There is evidence, however, that scientists themselves do not conceive of science in either fashion. Plutarch writes of Archimedes, the greatest scientific genius of antiquity: ". . . Archimedes possessed such a lofty spirit, so profound a soul, and such a wealth of scientific theory, that although his inventions had won for him a name and fame for superhuman sagacity, he would not consent to leave behind him any treatise on this subject, but regarding the work of an engineer and every art that ministers to the needs of life as ignoble and vulgar, he devoted his earnest efforts only to those studies the subtlety and charm of which are not effected by the claims of necessity." And of the famous engines of Archimedes he says: "To these he had by no means devoted himself as work worthy of his serious effort, but most of them were mere accessories of a geometry practiced for amusement." [9] To the layman it is incomprehensible that geometry should be practiced for amusement, but it is precisely this which marks the distinction between the layman and the geometer. For the geometer the joy of discovery is its own reward, and to one who has never experienced this rapture it will always seem a curious madness. Thales, the first Greek scientist, who fell into a well while gazing at the stars and was laughed at by a witty Thracian maidservant, is the proper representative of all science.

This madness of the scientist is curiously akin to the madness of the artist. Not only are the outward manifestations much the same, but even the inner ecstasy is similar. In the passage above, Plutarch speaks of the "subtlety and charm" of the proper studies of Archimedes. It is this aesthetic charm to which scientists most often confess,[10] and in fact this joy in the discovery of immediate truth is barely distinguishable from the artist's joy in aesthetic creation. If, as we have argued, science is done for the sake of this joyful apprehension, then science, like art, is a form of play, and their affinity is clear and unmistakable.

5. THE SERIOUSNESS OF PHILOSOPHY AND RELIGION

AFTER our initial division of activities into playful and non-playful we have been led to assign both art and science to the class of playful activities — a provisional decision which must be more carefully defended in later chapters. We must

---

[9] Cohen and Drabkin, *op. cit.*, pp. 315, 317.

[10] "The mathematician's patterns, like the painter's or the poet's, must be *beautiful;* the ideas, like the colour or the words, must fit together in a harmonious way. Beauty is the first test: there is no permanent place in the world for ugly mathematics." G. H. Hardy, *A Mathematician's Apology*, Cambridge, 1941, p. 25.

at this point return to philosophy and religion and ask of each, Is it playful or non-playful? And if non-playful, is it serious, in our sense of the word?

It is incongruous to describe religion as playful. If happiness is sought in religion, it is eventual, not immediate, happiness, and all consolation borrows its sweetness from the blessedness it anticipates. Religion, in fact, seems to be the prime example of a serious activity in our present meaning of the word; it is born of a passionate desire to achieve the well-being of oneself or others and is nourished by the hope that perfection of self is possible and not an empty dream. Consciousness of sin is not merely an awareness of imperfection but an aspiration toward perfection. Concern for self, whether self be defined as body or soul or the union of both, lies at the very heart of religion.

But what shall we say of philosophy? Philosophy is often conceived as a game which the philosopher plays with himself or his critics, a dialectical combat without intent or issue in which the victor, like a heavy-weight boxer, is fated to be vanquished by a younger adversary. Philosophers themselves often defend philosophy in these terms as a harmless kind of speculative exercise which may often anticipate science and teaches us in any case certain useful habits of thought. But even the lay mind senses that speculative philosophy differs in at least one important respect from speculative physics: it is concerned directly or indirectly with human happiness and human destiny. Kant contended that the three fundamental themes of metaphysics were God, freedom, and immortality, and the moral intent can be discerned at the base of every great speculative system. One of the greatest is, in fact, entitled ETHICA.

Dialectic may, in the hands of some philosophers, become merely a game, but then it merely reverts to the science from which it sprang — pure mathematics, and mathematics, as we have seen, is playful. Dialectic in the hands of a philosopher is used as an instrument to arrive at conclusions which lift philosophy above dialectic. Plato expressed this by saying that philosophical dialectic rises above the region of hypotheses or, as we would say, above the region of scientific "if . . . then . . ." statements, to a realm of categorical assertion. To the bystander who has no sense of the ultimate issues involved, the disputes of philosophers appear to be idle logic-chopping and logomachy. The philosopher is aware of the significance of the issues, but he is also aware that his conclusions can be reached and defended only by argument, and therefore to argument he gives himself heart and soul.

It is necessary then to conclude that both philosophy and religion are serious disciplines, in the sense that each is a group of activities which are done for the sake of the well-being of the agent or of other individuals affected by those activities. We need not consider at this point those respects in which philosophy and religion differ; it is enough to note the link which binds them together and which marks them off from art and science.

6. JUDGMENT

THE method of methodology we have been following, however imperfectly, permits us to make arbitrary divisions within the general class of activities and then insists that we accept the decision of common usage with regard to the assignment of a particular discipline to a given division. As methodologists we ask all the questions and common usage must provide all the answers. It is obvious in such procedure that the order of the questions and even their very nature is arbitrary. The arbitrariness is limited, however, by the fact that our questions must be of a sort to which common usage can provide some answer, and the class of activities finally cornered by the procedure must include all those accepted by common usage, but within these limits we have an assured and legitimate freedom. Instead of our initial division into human and non-human we could have begun with the division into playful and non-playful, or we could have begun with a distinction which I now propose to introduce: the distinction between those activities which involve an act of judgment (in a sense to be defined) and those which do not. It is convenient first to make the distinction and then to demonstrate how it may be incorporated into our previous scheme of division without making it the basis for a *primary* division.

Judgment may be defined with reference to the kind of sentence which expresses or corresponds to the judgment. Grammarians classify simple sentences into: statements, questions, expressions of desire, and exclamations. We are interested here in statements. Examples are: "Theaetetus sits," "John loves Mary," "Two is less than three." These are simple rather than compound sentences, and it is convenient to define "statement" more generally as follows: A given sentence will be called a "statement" if it makes sense to prefix the sentence by the expression: "It is the case that . . ." Thus "Woe is me!" or "The greatness that was Rome!" are not statements, whereas "Theaetetus flies" is a statement, since the sentence "It is the case that Theaetetus flies" makes sense, although we should ordinarily decide that it is false. According to our definition the following sentences are also statements:

If $2 + 1 = 3$, then 2 is less than 3.
2 is less than 3 or 2 is equal to 3 or 2 is greater than 3.

We can now define "judgment" as "that mental act which corresponds to, or is expressed by, a statement." The exact relation between a judgment and its corresponding statement is obscure, but there is one obvious difference: since a statement is a sentence, it can occur only *within* an act of perception or imagination, whereas a judgment is *itself* a mental act. Thus a judgment can occur without being itself perceived or imagined, and this is not true of a statement.

We shall say that an activity "involves judgment" when it eventuates ideally in an act of judgment. Leapfrog and politics, according to this definition, do not involve judgment, while the simple act of counting does. Mathematics and indeed science in general are perfect examples of activities which involve judgment, and the way is now clear to ask of each of our fundamental disciplines: Does it or does it not involve judgment?

The expression "involves judgment" is not wholly satisfactory to mark the distinction intended. The distinction is properly between those activities which aim at *ends* which literally involve judgment and those which do not. Thus the child in counting aims at a judgment expressed, for example, by "We are seven." The full-fledged mathematician aims at constructing a proof, say, for the statement that a given series of terms is convergent and has a specified sum, but such a proof is nothing but a complex statement of the form: "From certain presuppositions and definitions, it follows that this series of terms is convergent and has this particular sum." The experimental physicist aims at that occasion when he can triumphantly assert, "The specific gravity of this piece of metal is numerically such and such" or "The charge on the electron is (within the limits of experimental error) so many electrostatic units of electricity." In all these cases the activity cannot be completed (ideally) without an act of judgment expressed in a statement. It is exactly this which we mean when we use the phrase "involves judgment."

We must now ask of each of the other fundamental disciplines: Does it aim at an end which involves judgment, or more shortly, does it involve judgment? If science aims at the construction of certain kinds of judgment (or more exactly, at the pleasure which accompanies certain kinds of judgment), shall we say the same of art? The answer, according to common usage, is No. The products of sculpture and of musical art are not statements nor do they necessarily involve judgment in our sense of the word. One must not be misled by the fact that they do involve "aesthetic judgment," since aesthetic judgments are merely reactions of liking, disliking, or preference, and are therefore not judgments which can be expressed by statements as we have defined them. The proper words to express our aesthetic judgments are phrases such as "Bah!" or "How lovely!", and these are not statements. The sentence, "I like this picture," may, of course, express a judgment, but such a judgment springs from a sudden awareness of my *relation* to the picture. It is nothing but an awareness of my aesthetic reaction and is not identical with the reaction itself. To feel is not necessarily to be aware that one is feeling. Such awareness, since it is a genuine judgment, may be expressed by a statement. The situation is complicated by the fact that a sentence such as "I like this picture" may, in spite of its declarative form, be essentially an exclamation which expresses a genuine aesthetic judgment. Such cases are often revealed by the mode of utterance, for example, the vocal underlining of the word "like."

7. CREATION AND DISCOVERY

OUR conclusion is that art does not aim at judgment and that science does, but the exact relation between the two remains obscure. In order to clarify it we must go back to our previous admission that both are forms of play and mark out some of the main divisions of play. Art must then be assigned to one of these divisions and science to another.

One main division of play is that which makes things, and clearly many artistic activities fall within this division. But if by "things" we mean "physical objects," then singing and dancing will not fall within this division. If we agree, however, that by "things" we shall mean "physical objects or bodily movements," then it seems apt to say that art is a species of play which makes things. It is, in short, one form of creative play.

There are other forms of play, and rather than attempt to list them all by a rigorous "division by dichotomy" we shall fix on that form of play in which the characteristic pleasure attends an act of discovery. Hide-and-seek is an example of such discovery play, and the exploring of unfamiliar places, which affords such delight to children and adventurers, is another example. These are instances of discoveries of *things*, but there is another kind of discovery play in which one discovers relations between things, relations moreover which can be expressed in statements. The child who discovers that the word "Puff" in the magazine is the same word that appears in his primer is making this sort of discovery, and the pleasure accompanying the discovery is usually obvious and inordinate. If I have chosen examples from childhood play, it is only because I should like to insist that with such discovery play the child is making his first steps in science, and that science is that kind of play which attempts to discover the relations which hold between things, where by "things" I now mean not merely observable objects or qualities but also those entities which are the subject matter of mathematics and logic. In order to incorporate our previous remarks concerning judgment into this definition we shall agree that the relations between things discovered by science must be capable of being expressed in a statement. This excludes relations which can be merely felt or "apprehended," and we shall see that such relations do exist.

If art is a species of play which makes things or movements, it should now be clear that its end does not involve judgment in our sense of this phrase. Art may make and use judgments in its own creative activity, but the pleasure derived from the apprehension of a created object or movement is quite different from the pleasure which accompanies the discovery of a relation between things. Art does not make things or movements for the sake of using them or for the sheer pleasure of making them. Otherwise the blacksmith and the athlete would be artists. The blacksmith is often called an artist, but as we shall see this springs from the traditional confusion of art and craft. The artist makes things or movements for the sake of the pleasure he gets from the immediate sensuous (or imaginative) apprehension of them and for no other reason. It is in fact the apprehension of the completed and perfected object or movement which brings him his coveted reward of aesthetic pleasure or the humiliation of aesthetic pain.

What is of primary importance is that aesthetic apprehension is not an instance of judgment at all. It is rather pure perception—sheer *aesthesis*. The distinction between judgment and perception was clearly drawn by Plato in the THEAETETUS [11] in his argument that perception is not knowledge, since knowledge is impossible without judgment and the senses make no judgments. A sense organ perceives, but it does not make judgments about what it perceives, nor can diverse sense organs compare or contrast their perceptions. Plato concludes that judgment is a separate act of the "mind." What is important for our present purpose is that there is a type of experience, a pure perception or pure

[11] 184 B–186 E.

apprehension, in which our attention is wholly absorbed by the perceivable qualities of the object of our experience, with the result that all acts of judgment as such are suspended and we, attend merely to the immediate datum and the reactions it arouses in us. It is often said that in such moments we are adopting an "aesthetic attitude" toward the objects of our experience. This attitude is at any rate distinct from a practical, an analytical, or a scientific attitude. In such moments we are content to sense and feel; we make no plans and no judgments.

8. *JUDGMENT AND COMMITMENT*

By making a division within the realm of play we have attempted to justify our assignment of science to that class of playful activities which involve judgment and our exclusion of art from that class. We can now return to philosophy and religion and ask how each of these disciplines should be assigned. Our procedure will be analogous to that used in the case of science and art. We shall introduce arbitrary divisions in the general class of serious activities and attempt to locate philosophy and religion within certain of these subdivisions.

We have previously agreed that philosophy uses dialectic, but not for the sake of the pleasure of using it but as an instrument to discover or defend certain conclusions. These conclusions in turn are of the sort that have a bearing on the well-being of at least one individual. But dialectic manipulates statements and nothing but statements, and the conclusions to which dialectic leads must therefore be statements, that is, they are expressions of a final act of judgment. We must therefore agree that the conclusions aimed at by philosophy involve judgment and that they are prized and sought after by reason of their implicit bearing on the well-

being or happiness of some individual. "Pleasure is the highest good," "The self is a soul," "The self is the body" are
statements which express such philosophic conclusions. The
result is that philosophy, like science, is an activity which
involves judgment. Furthermore, it is an activity of discovery, but the discovery is not made for the sake of the
pleasure which accompanies it but for the sake of its bearing
on the well-being of some individual. We may rephrase this
by saying that philosophic discoveries are made for the sake
of their "moral implications." (I should prefer to use, instead of "moral," the older term "practical," but its meaning has been debased by utilitarianism and pragmatism.)

Philosophy then is a branch of that class of serious activities which attempt to arrive at certain conclusions, expressible in statements, for the sake of their moral implications.
What shall we say of religion? Does it aim at conclusions of
this sort? I do not believe that it does. Religion is done for
the sake of inducing a certain *disposition* of will, heart, soul,
or affections in ourselves or in others; it does not aim at simple judgments, whatever their moral implications. Religion,
like philosophy, aims ultimately at a condition of individual
well-being, but its immediate or penultimate end is a disposition of the self or will which is regarded as a necessary condition for attaining final happiness. All men at some time in
their life have what are usually called "religious experiences," but what marks the religious man and distinguishes
him from all others is that he welcomes and methodically in-
duces such experiences either in himself or in others. Nor
does he welcome these experiences for the sake of the pleasure
they bring, since they often disturb his complacency and ex-
pose his moral weaknesses. The method of religion is always
rhetorical rather than logical; it exhorts, commands, en-
treats, but it never argues. It appeals to the "heart" rather
than the head, to the will rather than the reason. It may use

the results and apparatus of reason, but it uses them, not to produce a rational conviction, but to produce a change of heart.

Our conclusion is that religion is not a discipline which involves judgment, since it does not aim, either ultimately or penultimately, at conclusions valued for their moral implications. It aims instead at a direct transformation of character which in turn is believed to lead inevitably to an even higher perfection. In so far as this transformation is accompanied by an act of dedication and resolution, it may be called a "commitment," and the distinction between philosophy and religion can be expressed by saying that the one involves judgment, the other commitment.

9. *IMMEDIATE AND TRANSCENDENTAL*

O U R previous analysis has shown us that art and science are both forms of play and that philosophy and religion are both serious. On the other hand science and philosophy are disciplines which involve judgment while art and religion do not. We shall now introduce a division which will reveal a new affinity of art and science and a corresponding bond uniting philosophy and religion.

The distinction arises in making a comparison of the statements of philosophy and science. It is characteristic of scientific statements that they are either immediately verifiable by perception or logical inspection or that one can deduce from them (by purely formal means) statements which can be so verified. Thus from the statements "All bodies on the surface of the earth are heavy" and "This is a body on the surface of the earth," I can deduce the statement "This body is heavy" and then proceed to verify this last statement by perception. The examples I have previously given of philosophical statements are not of this sort, how-

ever. There is no way in which I can verify by direct perception that pleasure is the highest good nor that the self is the
body, nor can I deduce from these statements any other statements which could be so verified. It is clear furthermore
that they cannot be verified by logical inspection. If philosophical statements were verifiable in the same fashion as
scientific statements, they would be merely a subclass of
scientific statements: those which are sought for the sake of
their bearing on our well-being.

There is no general agreement concerning the meaning of
the phrase "immediate experience," but if we agree to apply
the phrase only to "direct apprehension in sensation or imagination," then we can say that some appeal to immediate
experience is necessary in order to establish or confirm any
scientific statement. Philosophic statements on the other
hand cannot be established or verified by an appeal to immediate experience, and the evidence for their truth is therefore of some other sort. This distinction is admitted by all
those who seek the "elimination of metaphysics" on the
ground that metaphysical statements cannot be verified
either by logical inspection or direct perception and therefore say nothing significant. If science be called a "discipline
of immediacy" by reason of its appeal to immediate experience, then philosophy should be called a "transcendental
discipline," since philosophic statements refer to entities and
relations which cannot be identified in immediate experience, and therefore statements about them can never be
verified by such experience.

If our previous account of art is accepted, then art too
must be called a "discipline of immediacy," since without
direct apprehension by sensation or imagination no work of
art can be created or enjoyed. Aesthetic judgment, as a
matter of fact, arises as an emotional reaction from such
apprehension, but unlike scientific judgment it cannot be

expressed by a statement. Both aesthetic judgment and scientific judgment arise therefore from immediate experience, the first as a characteristic feeling of pleasure or pain, the second as a statement of fact.

The decision with respect to religion is much more difficult. The religious mystic is often regarded as the best example of the religious, [12] and mystical experience as the purest instance of immediate experience. It is characteristic of the mystic to deny, however, that what he experiences is describable in terms borrowed from sensation or imagination. He asserts that mystical knowledge "transcends" all sensation and imagination. What is important for our purpose is that the state of perfection of self at which all religion aims, even if it be regarded as a mystical union of the self and some being or entity other than the self, is still not immediate experience in our sense, since that entity with which the self desires to be identified is not to be apprehended by sense or imagination.

One reason then for declaring religion to be a "transcendental" discipline is that the state of well-being at which it aims is not an instance of immediate experience. There is another respect, however, in which religion is transcendental. We have seen that it does not eventuate in immediate experience, but it seems also not to arise from immediate experience. Our religious aspirations and needs seem not to be aroused by our sensory experience but to exist prior to such experience. It is in this sense that one can talk of a religious a priori, a disposition of the self which is not created by immediate experience and, as we have seen, cannot be satisfied by immediate experience. We cannot talk of religious a

[12] It is unfortunate that English has no unique terms for "the condition of being religious" or for "one who is religious." "Religiosity," for instance, is usually a term of reproach. Since religion is an activity, I have chosen to use the phrase "the religious" in the purely neutral sense of "one who does religion" without implying that such an individual is a member of any religious institution.

priori knowledge, but only of an a priori hunger or need which requires a satisfaction not of this world.

We have seen that philosophic statements cannot be verified by immediate experience, and if we agree that philosophic knowledge is the assurance that some philosophic statement is true, then we may also say that philosophic knowledge does not arise out of immediate experience. This does not mean that such knowledge is in the mind *before* experience, but merely that such knowledge is not attained by an appeal to immediate experience. How such knowledge is attained will be considered later in greater detail. We shall merely note that with respect to what such knowledge is *about* it is transcendental and with respect to its origin and conditions it is a priori.

The a priori appears therefore both in religion and philosophy but with significant differences. The religious a priori is a disposition of the self toward moral perfection which does not arise from immediate experience and is not satisfied by it. Since religion, however, as we have seen, does not involve judgment, the religious a priori does not give rise to religious *knowledge*. In the case of philosophy on the other hand the a priori appears as a transcendental ground for the knowledge at which philosophy aims, and such knowledge, since it neither arises from immediate experience nor can be verified by it, must be called a priori.

10. *CONCLUSION*

It is advisable now to construct a summary of our provisional conclusions in this chapter. We have discovered that each of our fundamental disciplines is an activity and indeed a human activity; that art and science are forms of play and disciplines of immediacy; that science in turn is linked with philosophy since both are disciplines which in-

volve judgment; that philosophy and religion are serious and
transcendental; and finally that religion is linked with art
since neither eventuates in judgment. These relationships can
be most conveniently diagrammed by constructing a simple
square with one discipline at each of the vertices. Then each
of the vertices is linked with adjacent vertices in the manner
we have just described. It will be noted that there are no links
connecting science and religion and none connecting art
and philosophy. With references to these traditional antagonisms our diagram can conveniently be called a "square of
opposition." It will be the task of the following chapters to
examine these antagonisms at greater length in the course of
constructing a unified and coherent account of each of the
four fundamental disciplines.

[THREE]

Art

1. *ART AND CRAFT*

THE argument of the preceding chapters has been founded on the apparent paradox that the definition of any fundamental discipline cannot be determined without specifying at the same time its relation to the other fundamental disciplines. We might add that it has been the intent of these chapters to demonstrate that the paradox in this case is specious and that such an assumption is inevitably forced upon us by the very nature of the problem. We shall now attempt to sketch in greater detail the nature of each of our disciplines as implied by our previous commitments. It will be convenient for the sake of concreteness to consider certain distinctions heretofore unmentioned, but our account will not pretend to completeness nor will the dimensions of this essay permit a reasoned defense of our assumptions.

The first supplementary distinction to be introduced is that of art and craft. Such a distinction is fundamental for any theory of art, but its importance for our inquiry is enhanced by the fact that a similar distinction — that of science and technology — is equally fundamental for a theory of science. Fortunately it is unnecessary to elaborate from the beginning a general account of craft and the characteristics which distinguish it from art. This has been done with admirable clarity by R. G. Collingwood in the second chap-

ter of his PRINCIPLES OF ART. It will be sufficient for our
purpose, however, to attend merely to the distinction between those activities which are done for the sake of an end
other than the activity and those which are done for the
sake of the activity itself or, more explicitly, for the sake of
the pleasure which accompanies the activity. I shall contend
that craft is a species of the first sort of activity and art of the
second. Aristotle in the beginning sentences of the NICO-
MACHEAN ETHICS distinguishes these two sorts of activities,
and in a parallel passage in the MAGNA MORALIA[1] gives building as an instance of the first and flute-playing as an instance
of the second. This agrees exactly with our intentions. He
insists, however, that all craft (*technē*) is a matter of making,
not of doing, and distinguishes making from doing on the
score that making has an end over and above the activity
itself, whereas doing does not.[2] Here again building is mentioned as an example of making and harp-playing as an
instance of doing. It would follow from these statements of
Aristotle that craft is always a kind of making and that art
(in our sense) is not. This conclusion is a matter of primary
importance and must be carefully scrutinized.

    First of all, it would follow from Aristotle's distinction
that architecture and poetry would be instances of making
while flute-playing and harp-playing would not, since Aristotle seems to assume that *what* is made is always a thing. He
assumes in other words that in all making what is made is
some thing distinguishable from the activity of making that
thing and that this thing is the end of that activity. But it is
clearly not necessary to assert that in all instances of making
the thing made is the end of the activity. The activity is not
always separable from the thing but is concretely the activity
of making *that* thing. In this sense the activity-of-making-a-
thing can be its own end. One *can* build a house for the sake

[1] 1211b.   [2] 1197a.

of building a house, and this instance is crucial in distinguishing the architect from the construction engineer.

Secondly, activities of doing (those which involve no physical products) can be done for the sake of something lying beyond the activity. Gymnastics can be done for the sake of health or beauty, flute-playing for the sake of honor or money. In other words the action itself can be a means, and the end can be a thing, as in the case of fishing, or another action, in the case of athletic training.

We may conclude that Aristotle's distinction between activities done for the sake of some end lying beyond themselves and those done for their own sake is not equivalent to the distinction between activities which make physical products and those which do not. It is the first distinction only which we propose to retain in distinguishing art and craft. Aristotle himself, as Collingwood has pointed out,[3] never distinguished between craft and art proper, and his analysis therefore merely provides him with distinctions *within* craft. If we do pursue our suggested distinction between art and craft, it is still significant to ask, Are there two *kinds* of art — art which makes and art which does not?

If "to make" means "to make a physical thing," then the answer is obvious. Architecture, sculpture, painting are arts of making; music, the dance, poetry are not. But if "to make" means "to create," then all the arts are arts of making. Some make things, others make patterns of sounds or movements, and in the latter case one must distinguish carefully between making sounds and movements and making (perhaps by writing) directions for producing such sounds or movements. The concrete work of art is still a pattern of sounds or movements in which (ordinarily) the composer is distinct from the performer and in which the former provides the plan or directive and the latter the execution. In our

[3] R. G. Collingwood, *The Principles of Art*, Oxford, 1938, p. 18.

subsequent discussion we shall retain this most general sense of the verb "to make" and will assert therefore that all art is a species of making. It will follow also that all craft is a species of making, and the distinction between the two is simply that art is done for its own sake, that is, it is a form of play, and craft is not. Craft is done always for the sake of some end lying beyond the activity of making.

This result is significant since it enables us, as Collingwood has shown,[4] to dismiss certain common conceptions of art by showing that according to such conceptions art is a species of craft. If anyone asserts that it is the end of art to represent physical things or ideal realities, to communicate thoughts or feelings, to teach or instruct, to amuse, to stimulate to thought or action, to improve by arousing useful emotions, he will in every instance be asserting that art is a kind of craft. The act of creation will be a means in every case to some end lying beyond itself. Thus it is unnecessary to examine singly each of these conceptions of art. They can be abolished at a stroke by showing that each presupposes art to be a form of craft.

2. *MAKING AND EXPRESSION*

THERE are two conceptions of art which are not dismissed by the preceding analysis which must still be distinguished from art proper. The first is the conception that art is expression and the second that it is self-amusement. The belief that art is some form of expression, whether of thought or of feeling or both, is axiomatic in most contemporary discussions. This is the theory, for example, to which Collingwood [5] is led by his distinction between art and craft, and it must be admitted that if, as he maintains, art is the expression of

---

[4] *Ibid.*, p. 32
[5] *Ibid.*, chap. VI.

emotions of which we are not clearly aware until they are expressed, then art is not a kind of craft. We have clearly no well-defined end in mind lying outside the activity itself.

The strength of this view lies in this, that it is able to explain the phenomenon of artistic "inspiration." Plato observed in the ION that the artist is mad and out of his mind at the moment of creation. This admission of possession, to which most artists will testify, is incompatible with the belief that the artist is coolly and deliberately and "craftily" plotting to achieve a clearly preconceived end. He doesn't *know* at the beginning how he is going to end. Hence the invocation to the Muses is not mere politeness. The artist in this case is apt to insist that he is in fact being used, as a means or tool, for the end which is the act of creation or expression.

Every theory of expression, however, must presuppose that *what* is expressed, whether it be thought or emotion, exists before it is expressed. Otherwise there is *creation* of emotion. If we are conscious of such thoughts or emotions before they are expressed, then the effort to express them is nothing more than an effort to find an appropriate means of expression, and this is a matter of skill, that is, of craft. If we are merely conscious that we have thoughts or feelings but are not clearly conscious what we think or feel, then it is no longer possible to assert that the feeling or thought expressed is identical with the feeling or thought of which we were vaguely conscious *before* the act of expression.

If we confine ourselves to the view that art is an expression of emotion, then according to this view art is an activity by means of which we discover what our feelings are and therefore, by our previous argument, what they were at some previous moment. Now it is possible, but by no means necessary, that we are impelled to create a work of art by some emotional excitement. We *may* do it on commis-

sion or for the sake of prestige or merely to keep our hand
in. In short, the romantic conception that the artist before
the act of creation is in an emotional "dither" must be given
up. The excitement we feel at the beginning may, as a matter of fact, come merely from an anticipation of the joys of
creation. Even if we admit that we are initially inspired by
certain non-aesthetic emotions such as hate or love or envy,
and this is quite possible, it still does not follow that what
we feel during the act of creation or at the end of it is identical with the emotion initially felt. In such cases we are apt
to confuse expression of emotion with discharge of emotion.
What is characteristic of such discharges is that at the end of
the activity of discharging one no longer feels the emotion
one initially felt. But literal *identity* of the two feelings is required by the theory.

We may admit that in certain instances of artistic creation, those which are accompanied by discharges of emotion,
our final emotional experience is "poorer" than our initial
experience, but if art is not merely discharge of emotion,
this final experience must also be richer than the initial experience. The activity of creation creates emotions; it does
not merely express or discharge them. There is a joy of
creation which does not exist before, and only in retrospect
after, creation. In particular there is the pure sensuous
pleasure which comes from the apprehension and manipulation of the medium. The excitement of seeing *this* combi-
nation of colors or *this* plastic contour, of hearing *this* pattern of sounds, cannot exist until the patterns exist, and the
patterns cannot exist until they have been created. The
patterns themselves may occur accidentally. The medium or
a jostling of one's elbow may produce effects which we never
intended but which on inspection we approve and incorporate in the finished product. The result is that emotion,
and not merely things, are created in the act of artistic crea-

tion. It is the failure to realize the importance of accident in artistic creation which finally condemns the conception of art as expression.

It would now appear that if art is not expression of feeling and if it is not identical with any form of craft, then it must be merely self-amusement. (To conceive the end of art as amusement of others would reduce it to craft.) If we should conceive of self-amusement as any activity which is done for the sake of the characteristic pleasure which accompanies it, then we seem to be forced to assert that art is self-amusement since it has no end beyond itself and is not expression. According to our previous definition of "play" we should then be asserting that self-amusement and play are identical. The terms are not always used synonymously, however, and the distinction seems to be this: one who is amusing himself is satisfied with *any* kind of pleasure, whereas anyone who plays seeks a determinate sort of pleasure. It will be convenient at least to use the words in this sense to mark this important distinction. Although the end of art is pleasure, it is not any kind of pleasure, but a specific kind, and we must now attempt to describe the characteristics of this pleasure in greater detail.

3. *ART AND PLEASURE*

I F art be considered as expression of emotion, then a good work of art is one in which some emotion is adequately or completely expressed. It would follow (as Collingwood has explicitly recognized [6]) that art is not concerned with any specifically aesthetic emotion since such emotions cannot be expressed. It also follows that art has nothing to do with beauty, if beauty produces in us purely aesthetic emotions, and if beauty be conceived as the object of love or desire, the

[6] *Ibid.*, pp. 116–17.

expressiveness of an art object has nothing to do with its
beauty. We do speak, however, of beautiful works of art, and
if we intend the word "beauty" to be taken in either of the
above senses, then this usage can only cast further doubt on
the adequacy of the view that art is expression.

If "beauty" be taken to mean "the object of love or
desire," as it is in Plato's SYMPOSIUM, then there is some
doubt that a work of art can be said to be beautiful. Joyce's
remarks in A PORTRAIT OF THE ARTIST AS A YOUNG MAN are
valuable on this point: "The feelings excited by improper
art are kinetic, desire or loathing. Desire urges us to possess,
to go to something; loathing urges us to abandon, to go from
something. The arts which excite them, pornographical or
didactic, are therefore improper arts. The aesthetic emotion
(I use the general term) is therefore static. The mind is
arrested and raised above desire and loathing." [7] The
customary distinction between the aesthetic attitude and the
practical attitude rests on the fact that when we take an
aesthetic attitude toward any object, we are content merely
to contemplate it, and we experience simultaneously a
miraculous suspension of all feelings of desire or revulsion.

An alternative definition of beauty appears in Plato's
GREATER HIPPIAS: "The beautiful is that which is pleasing
through hearing and sight." [8] Joyce quotes a similar definition from Aquinas: *Pulchra sunt quae visa placent*, which he
translates: "That is beautiful the apprehension of which
pleases" and adds, "He uses the word *visa* to cover aesthetic
apprehensions of all kinds, whether through sight or hearing
or through any other avenue of apprehension. This word,
though it is vague, is clear enough to keep away good and
evil which excite desire and loathing. It means certainly a

[7] *A Portrait of the Artist as a Young Man*, Modern Library, 1928, p. 240.
[8] 298 A. Unless otherwise stated, all translations of Plato in the present
volume have been taken from the translations in the Loeb Classical Library,
published by the Harvard University Press.

stasis and not a kinesis." [9] If either definition is accepted, it does not follow that only works of art will be beautiful, but it does follow that works of art *may* properly be called beautiful in certain instances and that in fact their excellence may depend on their beauty. This conclusion, however, as we have seen, would have to be denied by any theory of art as expression.

If we return now to our previous distinction between play and self-amusement on the grounds that play seeks a determinate kind of pleasure and self-amusement any sort of pleasure, then it now becomes clearer the kind of pleasure which art seeks and therefore the kind of play it is. The final pleasure which the artist seeks is the pleasure which comes from apprehension in Joyce's sense. But art, as we have seen, is also an activity of making. Therefore art is an activity of making which is done for the sake of the pleasure obtained from the apprehension of the object made. But this pleasure is characteristic of the activity itself and cannot be detached from it as a separate end. Art is therefore, as we agreed, a form of play. Stated more exactly, it is that form of play which makes things for the sake of the pleasure derived from the aesthetic apprehension of them.

4. SENSATION AND IMAGINATION

"AESTHETIC" is derived from the Greek word "aisthesis," which means "perception by the senses." We must now ask whether aesthetic apprehension is identical with sensory perception and if not, just how it is related to it. Plato's definition of beauty in the GREATER HIPPIAS suggests that aesthetic apprehension should be limited to the sensations of sight and hearing. These in fact are often called the "aesthetic senses." Aquinas's definition, as Joyce makes clear, allows for other "avenues of apprehension."

[9] *A Portrait of the Artist as a Young Man*, p. 243.

It is a curious fact that we almost never apply the word "beautiful" to objects perceived through senses other than sight and hearing. "The soup is beautiful" will ordinarily be taken to direct attention to the visual character of the soup. We do apply such words as "delicious" to tastes, however, and words such as "nice" to odors, and these words seem to indicate, as well as "beautiful," some intrinsic property of that which is sensed. It is therefore presumably a semantic accident which equates beauty with that which is pleasing through sight and hearing alone.

If we agree, however, that every kind of sensation can be represented within aesthetic apprehension, it does not follow that every sensation is aesthetic. Our everyday existence ordinarily gives us little opportunity for aesthetic apprehension, and we can express this by saying that in a routine activity, such as catching a train, our sensations are merely signs for mechanical and practical reactions and are therefore not aesthetic, or we may assert that we do have aesthetic experiences but that they are overwhelmed and outnumbered by other components of our experience.

The latter alternative would seem to be the more plausible one. We might expect by reason of the sheer ugliness, both visual and auditory, which surrounds the lives of most civilized men, that our senses would be completely numbed so that we literally did not perceive and feel. But even the commuter is sensitive to the humidity, and this by our previous agreement can be called aesthetic apprehension. Most of what he does sense otherwise is sensed merely as signs to direct his attention to something else, but it is comforting, if not wholly plausible, to believe that some remnant of sheer sensibility remains. If his attention were completely focused on these components of his ordinary experience, as it is apt to be in the instance of humidity, we should be forced to describe his experience as aesthetic apprehension. It is implausible, in other words, that aesthetic apprehension should involve a different sort of sensation from the everyday variety. Aesthetic apprehension is actually pure sensation unalloyed by thinking or planning. It is complete and utter absorption in immediate sensory content, and it is an inscrutable law of our nature that absorption in some sensory contents is accompanied by pleasure and absorption in others by pain. It is the pleasure and pain arising from such pure sensation which we must call "aesthetic pleasure" and "aesthetic pain," and it is the presence of this pleasure and this pain which determines our application of the words "beautiful" and "ugly."

We must now ask whether we must restrict aesthetic apprehension to sensation alone or whether we should not agree that certain imaginative experiences are also instances of such apprehension. We may not agree with Hobbes' famous characterization of imagination as "decaying sense," but it does at least apply to memory, and remembering is merely a kind of imagining. The traditional distinction is, I believe, between reproductive and productive imagination. It is again a psychological fact that when the reproductive imagination or memory presents us with the memory image of some pure sensation, then aesthetic emotions similar to those initially felt are aroused by, or accompany, this image. We do not merely remember the aesthetic emotions; we re-experience them. The point is, there can be absorption in content provided by memory, and such absorption is apt to produce aesthetic emotions similar to those attending the initial experience.

If this holds good for the reproductive imagination, why should it not apply to the productive imagination? Images created by the imagination can be attended to in the same way that we attend to memory images or to sensory content. There can be in short the same sort of absorption in imaginative content that we experience with respect to sensory content. The councils of Homer's gods can be (almost) as vividly apprehended as the meetings of the Security Council and with the same detachment. It is characteristic of imagination that it is always an imitation of sense. It is again a psychological fact that the images provided by the productive imagination do produce in us when we attend to them emotions of pleasure and pain similar to those produced in pure sensation and memory. We are entitled to assert therefore that aesthetic apprehension is complete absorption in sensory or imaginative content, where imaginative content is intended to include that provided by memory. Aesthetic emotions are emotions arising from, or accompanying, such apprehension.

5. *ART AND KNOWLEDGE*

WE have attempted to describe that sort of pleasure at which art aims, and we have found it to be the pleasure which accompanies aesthetic apprehension. It should be noted, of course, that in many instances there are other pleasures present too: the pleasure which comes from the discharge of emotion, the pleasure which comes merely from the activity of making, the pleasure which comes from the awareness that one is functioning as an artist. These pleasures, however, either are not always present in every instance of artistic creation or they are not characteristic of art alone. They cannot enter therefore into the account of pleasure by which art is defined.

We must now consider aesthetic apprehension more carefully and attempt to discover how it is related to what we call knowledge. It is useful at this point to adopt Bertrand Russell's distinction [10] between "knowledge of things" and

[10] Cf. *The Problems of Philosophy*, Oxford, 1948, p. 44.

"knowledge of truths," since we do seem to use the term "know" in these two main senses. If someone tells me that he knows Venice, this means ordinarily that he has perceived by sight at least some parts of Venice. If he tells me that he knows Mr. X, this means also that he has perceived Mr. X (or some parts of him). On the other hand if he tells me that he knows that two and two is four, he is not merely *acquainted with* something, but knows something *about* two and four, that is, that they are related by this simple equation. He knows, in other words, *that* a certain relation holds between 2 and 4, but he is not simply acquainted with this relation or with two or four.

The difference between these two cases may be expressed, as we have indicated in Chapter Two, by saying that judgment is involved in all knowledge of truths and it is not involved in knowledge of things. The phrase "knowledge of things," however, is not wholly adequate to denote knowledge of that which is merely given to our consciousness, and it is better perhaps to use Russell's expression "knowledge by acquaintance." We do not wish to suggest, that is, that such knowledge is literally only of things since it may be knowledge of anything immediately present to our consciousness, for example, blueness or twoness. "To know X" then means merely "to be aware that X was at one time, or is now, immediately present to my consciousness." Now what is given to us in aesthetic apprehension is given to us immediately, although it may not be the only sort of content given to us immediately. Aesthetic apprehension is, at any rate, an instance of knowledge by acquaintance, and as such it must be carefully distinguished from knowledge of truths.

We have previously agreed that aesthetic apprehension should include imaginative apprehension, and it follows from our previous statements that imagination also can provide us with knowledge by acquaintance. If we are asked "Acquaintance with what?" we can only reply, "With that which the imagination sets before us." Just as the historical imagination enables us to become acquainted with Cleopatra and Caesar and Napoleon, so the artistic imagination enables us to become acquainted with Oedipus and Hamlet and Tonio Kröger. Students of literature often speak of the characters in a novel or a play as if they were as "real" as the author or themselves. We become acquainted with real persons by observing them; we become acquainted with literary characters (or things or events) by attending to the images aroused by written or spoken words and the movements of actors on a stage or screen.

What is presented to us, however, by the senses or the imagination is always particular. It may be considered a symbol of what is "universal" or "quintessential," but *in itself* it is always particular, and aesthetic apprehension of it is always apprehension of it as it is in itself. Aristotle, with the obtuseness characteristic of scientific men in the presence of art, is responsible for much of the confusion on this point in literary circles by reason of his insistence that the statements of poetry are universal in the sense that they are statements "of what such or such a kind of man will probably or necessarily say or do — which is the aim of poetry, though it affixes proper names to the characters." [11] Plato had shown that this is precisely what art can *not* do; it cannot present us with true or probable or necessary universal statements. Are the statements about Oedipus in OEDIPUS TYRANNUS statements about "such or such a *kind* of man?" Clearly not. They are statements merely about Oedipus, and we are not entitled to deduce from them any statements about any other literary personage nor about any real person and therefore nothing about Man. It is sometimes said, in imitation of Aristotle, that literature portrays for us the *possibilities* of human na-

[11] *Art of Poetry*, ed. by W. Hamilton Fyfe, Oxford, 1940, p. 25.

ture, but this is certainly not equivalent to asserting that literature describes for us human nature as it *is* nor as it is apt to be. Such a statement probably intends to assert merely that literature enables us to know by acquaintance imaginary characters which imitate or resemble actual human beings. Gide has observed that "art can only live and have its being in the particular." [12] If this is true, as we contend, then any attempt to introduce universality into art in order to express philosophic or scientific truth can only result in producing bad art — or something other than art.

If art is unfitted, by its necessary dependence on sensation and imagination to give us universal truths about anything, it might nevertheless be able to present us with particular truths. Thus it might be contended that ULYSSES contains an exact description of Dublin, that WAR AND PEACE gives us a vivid and perfect picture of life in the aristocratic families of nineteenth-century Russia, that Hugo in LES MISÉRABLES tells us all we could possibly want to know about the sewers of Paris. Usually, it must be admitted, such statements are made by individuals who are not in a position to pass on their accuracy. If one's knowledge of life in aristocratic families in nineteenth-century Russia is obtained from Tolstoy, then it is natural to assert also that his account is accurate and exact. What one *means* presumably is that his account is vivid and detailed, and this applies equally well to the other instances above.

The same remarks apply to all instances of representation in painting and sculpture. A painting called "Marie Antoinette" is implicitly a statement of the form, "Marie Antoinette looked like this." If the subject did "look like this," then the artist has actually given us knowledge *about* the subject. It is easy to assume, however, as Plato would remind us, that because a painting looks like something or someone

[12] *If It Die*, tr. by D. Bussy, Random House, 1935, p. 198.

that the artist has given us knowledge *about* something or someone. Such knowledge could not be verified unless we had independent knowledge of that something or someone. Again vividness of presentation is confused with accuracy of representation.

It is unnecessary to go through these arguments in detail. One need only ask in the presence of particular truths in "art-objects": Is this truth essential to the character of this thing as an art-object? Or, more generally, must every work of art contain particular truths? Now there are at least some instances of architecture, music, painting, sculpture, poetry which are by common usage admittedly works of art which do not contain any particular (or universal) truths. We can conclude that what makes any object a work of art has nothing whatsoever to do with its truthfulness.

Our result could have been derived somewhat differently by noting simply that aesthetic apprehension can give us only knowledge by acquaintance, whereas knowledge of truths demands an act of judgment which issues explicitly or implicitly in a statement. We may contrast if we wish "the given" with "interpretations of the given." What is significant is that art is content to provide us merely with data for aesthetic apprehension. It does not intend or insist that we make any interpretations of these data nor any statements about the relations which hold between them. This is the function of science. Art is content to provide the materials for aesthetic contemplation, and only those incapable of ecstatic absorption in "the given" are apt to insist that it do more.

We may conclude then that art does present us with knowledge, but it is knowledge *of* things, not knowledge *about* things. This distinction is important since it is quite true to say that art can extend the range and depth and richness of our experience without adding an iota to our information or factual knowledge. It is well known, of course, that it *seems* to give us factual knowledge, and this is what horrified Plato and must horrify anyone who realizes the extent to which imaginative literature determines our conception of our duties and the nature of the social and physical worlds we inhabit. The only antidote against the harmful misconceptions produced by imaginative literature is, as Plato remarks,[13] a knowledge of its real nature. The artist, Nietzsche said, is a liar. The world of appearance, in which the artist lives and moves and has his being, seems to the non-artist more "real" than the actual world. He has forgotten unfortunately what he knew very well as a child, that a story need not be true to be interesting.

6. *ART AND MORALITY*

WE have concluded that the artist's absorption in the world of appearance, in the sense that it is the world which immediately *appears* to him, makes him indifferent to the problem of stating precisely the relations which hold between the experienced elements of that world, that is, it makes him indifferent to truth. For the same reason it makes him indifferent to the bearing of that world on our moral well-being. If the scientist is possessed with an overpowering desire to know which leads him in where the moralist fears to tread, the artist is possessed with a comparable desire to *experience*, regardless of the consequences, and he will insist on experiencing the evil with the good. In fact, what is evil or novel or horrible is apt to be more exciting as a theme or subject than what is good or normal or conventional. Plato observes [14] that tragedies are not constructed by presenting the adventures of intelligent or temperate characters.

[13] *Republic* 595 B.
[14] *Republic* 604 E.

The criticisms of art by the moralist are mainly of two sorts. The first criticism is that we cannot portray or experience evil without becoming evil. According to this view, the attempt to describe literally or imaginatively the interior of a brothel would give rise to some sort of moral contamination as inevitably as the attempt to describe on the spot the activities of a leper colony would produce physical infection. It would follow furthermore according to this view that we could be contaminated by our own creations, and that Shakespeare and Aeschylus, in so far as they are the creators of Lady Macbeth and Clytemnestra, were infected by their own products.

The contention of the moralist is in fact that the artist in the midst of evil cannot remain an artist. His humanity, that is, his humanness, betrays him in the midst of temptation, and he succumbs to the allurements of evil, as Delacroix succumbed to the physical charms of his models. Now this contention of the moralist is equivalent to denying that art is possible, since it asserts that it is impossible to maintain in the presence of evil an attitude of complete aesthetic detachment. It implies that dramatic sympathy with a literary character entails some moral approbation. It is important to realize, however, that this view is not incompatible with the definition of art to which we have been led. It asserts not only that most men cannot be artists, but that no one can.

We must in all honesty concede that most men cannot be artists, and for this reason, as Plato knew, experience of works of art can actually be harmful to them. It is equally impossible for any one individual to be an artist *all* the time nor are all his productions works of art. This does not prevent us, however, from recognizing art when we see it, nor does it make the contrast less sharp between art and pornography or between art and moral exhortation. The result is the paradox that if any one is corrupted by a work of art, he is corrupted by reason of the fact that he is *not* an artist. If it were a genuine work of art and if he looked at it with the eyes of an artist, he would come through the experience of it unscathed and serene.

The first complaint of the moralist, as we have seen, may be expressed in this form: No man can be consistently an artist. His human weaknesses war against the Olympian detachment required of the true artist with the result that he is in some degree always corrupted by his experiences as an artist or a spectator. He cannot read certain pages of Aristophanes or Rabelais without becoming vulgarized, nor Bocaccio or Chaucer without becoming in some degree libidinous. The first complaint is, in other words, as much a complaint against ourselves as against art. The second complaint is, however, a complaint against art alone. Even if this miraculous detachment of the artist *could* be maintained, so runs the indictment, it is still a danger, since it deflects our attention from what should be our sole concern — the salvation of our own souls. Indifference to good and evil becomes in this indictment evil in itself. Thus the moralist either finds it impossible to believe that the artist is really indifferent to good and evil or if he finds that he is, he is shocked by his callousness.

This second complaint may be regarded as an instance of the confusion produced by what we have previously called "polemic methodology." Polemic methodology, it may be remembered, attempts to show that the method of some one discipline is better than that of some other (or all others). In this instance the moralist, who is dedicated to the improvement of himself (and presumably of others), is merely complaining that the artist is not so dedicated. The artist in his turn might insist that only a life devoted to the pursuit of the riches offered to us by the senses and imagination is worth living and look with contempt on the blubberings and spiritual hypochondria of the moralist. He might point out that just as the hypochondriac's concern for health may become a bar to his enjoyment of it, so the moralist's concern with moral perfection may prevent him from attaining it.

There is an issue here which must be fairly met: Is concern for moral perfection itself an ingredient in such perfection? No definite answer can be given without some agreement about the meaning of "moral perfection," but it is important to observe that the answer to this question need not be Yes. If religion and philosophy are, as we have maintained, practical and therefore instrumental disciplines, then they and the attitudes they inculcate are valuable only as a means to something else. But moral perfection, if anything, must have intrinsic value. What value it has therefore must depend on aspects which are not purely religious or philosophic. By our account art and science can provide values which are intrinsic, since each is done for its own sake. These activities must be included therefore as components in any account of "happiness," as Aristotle was well aware. Happiness, if it is to exclude the pleasures of knowledge and the riches of aesthetic experience, is no longer recognizable. It is possible therefore that art and science, although they are not concerned with the attainment of moral perfection, are still important components of that perfection.

The fundamental problem is: Are they the only components? Religion and philosophy ordinarily refuse to be designated as practical or instrumental disciplines. Religion in particular would insist that happiness must include as a component a certain disposition of the will in addition to the pleasures of sense and knowledge, and philosophy argues for the intrinsic value of philosophic insight. Without examining these claims in detail we can at least assert this much: that a life lived without concern for moral perfection is unlikely to achieve it. If we don't desire virtue nor recognize it when we find it, then if we have it, we possess it by virtue of a kind of "divine dispensation," as Plato observes in the MENO.[15] If religion and philosophy be regarded as the means to virtue, it is still true that in willing the end we also will the means. From this point of view a perfect life must contain moments of religious devotion and philosophic insight, even though we exclude these from our account of "happiness." Furthermore, if happiness should properly be ascribed only to a life, as Aristotle recommends, and not to portions of it, then we can say that happiness must include religious and philosophic components. The perfect life then is a proper blend of the values provided by our four fundamental disciplines, in which religion and philosophy serve as means for the achievement of virtue, and art and science as a portion at least of its actual realization.

[15] 99 E.

[FOUR]

Science

1. *SCIENCE AND TECHNOLOGY*

O U R account of science must begin with a clear distinction between science and technology, just as we began our discussion of art with a distinction between art and craft. One can, in fact, state the relationships involved in the form of a simple proportion: as art is to craft, so is science to technology. Similarly, if the confusion of art and craft is the fundamental error of aesthetics, the confusion of science and technology is the fundamental error of the philosophy of science.

This confusion is only natural in our own civilization where we are surrounded by things which would not exist without the use of scientific knowledge, but the confusion itself has deep historical roots. It springs from the tendency of the early Greek physicists and mathematicians to identify what we call empirical physics with technology and then repudiate both. Proclus, in his summary of Greek mathematics,[1] says that according to a common conception mechanics is a "division of the study of material objects perceived by the senses," and he includes under the term "the manufacture of engines useful in war" and "the manufacture of wonderful devices." Archimedes, as we have seen, regarded "the work of an engineer and every art that

[1] M. R. Cohen and I. E. Drabkin, *A Source Book in Greek Science*, p. 5.

ministers to the needs of life as ignoble and vulgar" and
presumably considered only his theoretical researches scientific. Mechanics, as defined by Proclus, would then be
ignoble and vulgar. This conclusion was supported by the
conception of Plato and his followers, who determined most
of the thinking *about* science until the seventeenth century,
that empirical science was not genuine knowledge and therefore should not strictly be called science. The term "science"
was applied only to pure mathematics, theoretical physics,
and theoretical astronomy. All that was needed to overthrow
this conception of science was the demonstration in the
sixteenth and seventeenth centuries that observation and
experiment could provide genuine knowledge and were in
fact the only methods by which certain problems could be
solved. In such an atmosphere of empiricism it was easy to
conclude that the term "science" ought to be reserved for
empirical science alone and that pure mathematics, for example, ought to be lumped with metaphysics, as in Bacon's
ADVANCEMENT OF LEARNING,[2] or should be regarded merely
as a tool for science proper. What is important is the fact that
although empirical science rather than pure science was now
regarded as science proper, empirical science was still not
distinguished from technology, and Bacon's plea that science
must minister to the needs of life and can only be justified
if it does, made such a distinction difficult for subsequent
generations.

In general, all attempts to "justify" science have grown
out of misconceptions of its nature or have themselves
produced such misconceptions. The first important justification was announced by Plato. We may call it the "educational justification" of science. Science, according to Plato,
has no intrinsic value. It is valuable only as a means to
dialectic and the contemplation of certain kinds of "higher"

[2] Bk. II, viii, 1.

realities. After recommending that in harmonics one should ascend to "generalized problems and the consideration which numbers are inherently concordant and which not and why in each case,"[3] a recommendation which transforms harmonics into theory of numbers, he observes that such an undertaking is "useful for the investigation of the beautiful and the good, but if otherwise pursued, useless." He adds comments to the effect that most mathematicians are not dialecticians and therefore presumably never escape the charge of pursuing a useless activity. Mathematics, according to Plato, can produce in us a disciplined mind and a harmonized soul, it can teach us the secrets of "abstract" thinking, it can lead us to distinguish the sensible and the supersensible, and finally lead us to the contemplation of the higher Forms, but if it is not pursued for the sake of these ends, it must be considered useless. It would then be, like art, a kind of play, although Plato does not draw this inference.

Plato attempted to justify science on the ground that it could be used to remake men, Bacon on the ground that it could be used to remake nature for the advantage of men. Both would agree that if mathematics were pursued merely for the sake of amusement, as Archimedes believed, then it would have to be considered "useless," and Bacon is particularly eloquent on the theme of the fruitlessness of traditional science. According to the Platonic theory, science can benefit only those who *do* it, and there is a laudable humanitarianism in Bacon's insistence that science must be used for the benefit of all. What Bacon failed to see is that it is the function of science to make discoveries, and that another art or discipline is required to supervise the *use* of such discoveries. There is a distinction, in short, between pursuing knowledge for the

[3] *Republic*, 531 C.

sake of the pleasure of discovery and pursuing it as a means of solving a practical problem.

We have defined play as any activity which is done for the sake of the characteristic pleasure which accompanies it and have argued that art is a kind of play. Craft on the other hand is an activity of making which is done for the sake of a clearly preconceived end lying beyond the activity itself. The activity of making in this case is a means only and is not valued for any intrinsic characters it may possess. It is possible now to discriminate two kinds of discovery connected by a similar relation. There is, in the first place, discovery pursued for the joy of discovery, and secondly, there is discovery pursued as a means to a clearly preconceived end lying beyond the act of discovery itself. The first is science, the second technology.

The distinction between the two in concrete cases is not easy, since the result of every scientific discovery *can* be used as a means to something lying beyond it, and many, if not all, technological achievements include as subordinate phases the solution of theoretical problems which rival in complexity and significance the problems of pure science. It is not surprising then that scientific amateurs and philosophers should have confused science and technology just as their colleagues in aesthetics have confused art and craft. The craftsman *may* become excited by the aesthetic qualities of the forms he is producing and exist for this brief instant as an artist; so the technologist may be intrigued by a "puzzle" which occurs in the course of his work and, abandoning himself to the joy of discovery, become for this brief moment a scientist. It is not surprising that the terms "scientist" and "technologist" should be confused when they may both be applied to the same man. What is important is that even if such a man can legitimately be considered both a scientist and a technologist, what makes him a scientist is not what makes him a technologist. The analogy with the distinction between art and craft is thus exact.

The geometrical proportion stated above would lead us to assert that science is an activity of discovery pursued for the sake of the pleasure which accompanies the activity of discovery, just as art is an activity of making which is pursued for the sake of the pleasure which accompanies the aesthetic apprehension of what is being made. Craft, we have argued, is an activity of making which is done for the sake of some clearly preconceived end lying beyond the activity itself and to which the activity serves as a means. Before we compare craft and technology, however, this end must be stated more precisely, since, if we take our statement as a definition of craft, it is too broad. A carpenter may make a table for the sake of the money he expects to receive from the sale of it, but it is certainly not in virtue of such a relation of means and a preconceived end that we call him a craftsman. A locksmith may make a key at gunpoint, but this seems not to be an instance of craftsmanship, or at any rate it is not merely craftsmanship, although there is an activity of making which serves as a means to a preconceived end lying beyond the activity. What seems to be required to make our account of craft more precise is the recognition that the completed construction of the object (or movement) which is to be made is itself the clearly preconceived end or that the object or movement is itself a means to such an end. A boy who makes a chicken coop to escape his mother's anger is not a craftsman in virtue of this relationship of means and end, but if he makes it to such and such specifications or if he makes it to keep his pet chickens out of the garden, then he is a craftsman. Even in those cases in which the object made is a means to a more remote end, it is still obvious that it is itself a proximate end at one stage of the construction.

If the analogy of craft and technology holds good, we should now be able to say that technology is an activity of discovery which is done for the sake of some clearly preconceived end lying beyond the activity itself and to which the activity serves as a means. The analogy, however, goes even further. Just as craft institutes a process of making in order to achieve a preconceived end, the object or movement which is to be made, so technology posits its immediate end which is a condition or state of "knowing how." The technologist institutes a process of inquiry in order to know how to solve a predetermined problem, that is, the problem is given in advance and he attempts to make those discoveries and marshal that information which will enable him to say finally: I know how to do this, or make this, or avoid this. There is, of course, a linkage here of successive "knowing hows," so that knowing how to do A may lead to knowing how to do B and so on, just as there is a corresponding hierarchy of crafts. It is obvious, of course, that knowing *that* such and such is the case may also enable one to know *how*. The conclusion is that the technologist knows always for the sake of knowing how and never for the sheer joy of discovery or the moral implications of the knowledge obtained. In this respect he differs from the scientist and the philosopher.

There are certain important implications of this conception of technology. First of all, it does not follow that anyone who makes discoveries is a scientist, nor does it follow that anyone who makes discoveries that interest a genuine scientist is himself a scientist, just as a child is not considered an artist by reason of the fact that his painting is exciting to an artist. We need to know something of the *way* in which the discovery was made before we can call it scientific, just as we must know something about the way in which a picture was created before we can be certain it is a work of art. There must be some evidence, external or internal to the painting, that it was made by someone who was aware of its aesthetic significance. Likewise there must be some evidence in the case of a given discovery that the discoverer was aware of the intrinsic importance of the fact discovered, and by "intrinsic importance" I mean merely its *logical* relation to other facts. This does not preclude the possibility of scientific accidents, since such occurrences are accidents merely because the resultant knowledge did not function as a *preconceived* end, and they are scientific because their discoverer was aware of their intrinsic importance.

Secondly, it follows that the distinction between science and technology does not correspond to any distinction between types of subject matter. According to our conception, a man who observes and records faithfully the activities of a dung beetle merely "to satisfy his curiosity" must be considered a scientist, while the physicist who makes a careful study of matrix algebra *merely* for the sake of its applications in quantum mechanics or the art dealer who makes a careful study of Italian primitives *merely* that he may not be taken in by a forgery are both technologists. The difference between the scientist and the technologist is principally a difference of attitude, not of subject matter, nor, it may be added, of apparatus. Archimedes did science in his bath; Rutherford said he could experiment at the North Pole.

2. *SCIENCE AS DISCOVERY OF RELATIONS*

DISCOVERY undertaken for the sake of the peculiar pleasure which accompanies the act of discovery must then be considered science proper, but we must now attempt to make the meaning of "discovery" in this statement rather more precise. We have observed previously that a scientist is not a scientist by reason of his discovery of things, in the sense that he becomes acquainted with things, otherwise we should have to call every explorer a scientist. The scientist discovers, not things, but relations between things. "Things" must be taken here in the widest possible sense as "any object of consciousness." The distinction can be clarified if we take the example of the discovery of Neptune. In what sense is Leverrier (or Adams) the discoverer of Neptune? Neither was the first to *see* it through a telescope, since Galle to whom Leverrier sent his results, was the first to discover it in this sense. What Leverrier and Adams discovered was this: that *if* the observed perturbations of Uranus were correct and *if* the laws of Newtonian mechanics held for every body in the solar system, then there must exist some *other* body with such and such a position in the heavens which produced these perturbations. This is merely an "if . . . then . . ." proposition, but it constitutes the essence of their discovery, and the importance of it is not affected by Galle's observational discovery of the pin point in the sky which was to be called "Neptune." I do not wish to deny that it is important that scientific predictions be confirmed by observation but rather to affirm that an activity may legitimately be called good science even though the predictions to which it leads are not exactly true. Otherwise we should have to call Newton a bad astronomer since we know now that Newtonian mechanics is not exactly applicable to all astronomical phenomena. What we need to know is the *method* by which the scientist in question reaches his results, since this, if it is unsuccessful in one case, promises nevertheless to be successful in others. Leverrier was a scientist by virtue of "the way in which his mind worked." The actual discovery of Neptune must have been less exciting to him than to Galle; if he had checked his computations carefully, the discovery assured him merely that he had chosen the right assumptions, but it would not have occurred to him or to any of his contemporaries to doubt this.

In order to clarify our statement that "science is the activity of discovering relations between things" we must apply it to several concrete instances. A boy who finds a spider in the woods is not for that reason a scientist, but if he exclaims "This is the same spider I saw at Grandma's house!" then the activity which led to that exclamation must be called scientific, even though the conclusion might be wrong. If the boy becomes a biologist when he grows up, he learns to make more systematically the same kind of comparison made in this simple instance. The method is known as the method of classification, and the principle of it is to note the relations which hold between one thing and some other things. It is by virtue of such activity that an individual is located within a species, a species within a genus, and so on.

The boy in our illustration may say simply "This spider is red." This statement is still a comparison, since the intent is either to contrast the color of this spider with that of some other or to compare the color of this spider with that of some other object. It is equally obvious that a statement such as "This spider's body is much bigger than his head" is also a statement of a relation, although it does not refer to any other object. The relations then which are to be noted in scientific discovery are of various sorts: relations between things, relations between the properties possessed by things, relations between the parts (including properties) of one thing. It is possible, of course, to regard relations between things as reducible to relations between the properties "possessed" by things, but this is hardly necessary for our purpose.

If "thing" can mean, however, "any object of consciousness" or even more narrowly "anything sensed or imagined," then sentences and statements are things, likewise the parts of sentences. The activity of determining the relations which hold between sentences or between parts of sentences or between sentences and their parts is then scientific. It constitutes a good portion indeed of traditional grammar and logic. One of the specific tasks of logic, of course, is to isolate and clarify certain general kinds of relations which occur in sentential analysis. It differs from mathematics in this: that mathematics is concerned, not with these general types of relations between sentences, but with relations between certain general types of sentences. This usually appears as a relation between a certain set of sentences, called "postulates," to another set called "theorems." What pure mathematics is attempting to discover is simply the totality of relations which hold between sentences of a certain given kind, and these relations must themselves be expressed in sentences.

It was necessary to qualify the previous statement by the use of the word "pure" since mathematical statements can be "interpreted" in such a way that they become statements about imaginary or sensible things, that is, they become statements of the relations which hold between imaginary things or between sensible things. Such statements can, of course, be confirmed or disconfirmed by an appeal to sensation or imagination. Mathematics, as a body of interpreted statements, becomes now something more than a study of the relations between general types of sentences; it becomes also a study of the relations which hold between the "things" introduced by the interpretation. We have indeed a new problem: that of determining the relation which holds between the initial uninterpreted statements and the imaginary or sensible things denoted by the interpreted terms. This is the problem which appears, for example, when we attempt to use the propositions of geometry in surveying or the solutions of differential equations in empirical physics. Pure mathematics seeks merely to determine the relations which hold between certain uninterpreted sentences. If we assert further that these sentences state relations between certain imaginary or sensible elements, then we are committed to a further study of the relation of our uninterpreted sentences to the factual relations which hold between the "things" of our interpretation. In the case of surveying and mathematical physics such a study usually reminds us that the interpretation of mathematical statements in terms of sensible elements and relations can never be *exactly* carried out, and we usually express this by saying that physics is only an approximation to the exact situation described by the sentences of mathematics.

It is important to note, however, that "approximate" interpretations are used, not merely in applied mathematics, but also in what is usually called "pure mathematics." It is customary in analytic geometry to discuss certain types of algebraic equations as formulae for the construction of geometrical loci, that is, one asserts that to every set of values of the variables which satisfy the equation, there exists exactly one point which has those coördinates. A similar assumption is made in discussions of differential equations, where solutions of such equations correspond to curves and surfaces. I am not denying that exact interpretation of algebraic or differential equations can be made in terms of points and certain undefined relations between points, but I am merely asserting that in practice the mathematician himself often refers to an "approximate" interpretation in terms of sensible or imaginable points as a purely heuristic device in discussing his formal equations. Strictly speaking, the sequence of equations which he finally writes down are merely "strings of marks" so arranged that any member of the sequence follows from the preceding members of the sequence by the use of (non-arbitrary) rules of logical inference. What the mathematician discovers therefore is merely that a certain relation holds between certain strings of uninterpreted marks, although by virtue of his use of certain "approximate" interpretations he seems to have discovered something about the relations which hold between the elements of this interpretation.

We could introduce other instances to illustrate the point that science is the discovery of the relations which hold between things immediately apprehended in sensation or imagination, but for the present it is enough to note that the method of classification, which is so fundamental in the descriptive biological sciences, can be subsumed under this general account and that the method of pure and applied mathematics and of mathematical logic is also an instance of it. I am assuming that what we are talking about in mathematics or mathematical logic are elements which are sensed or imagined and that they cannot be apprehended in any other way. This means, of course, that the sentences of mathematics and mathematical logic are apprehended in the same way. It does not imply, however, that the logical *relations* discovered to hold between these sentences must themselves be apprehended by sensation or imagination. It is enough for our purpose to assert that all the *elements*, between which we attempt to discover relations in the act of scientific discovery, are themselves apprehensible by sense or imagination. It is for this reason that we have called science a "discipline of immediacy."

3. *SCIENCE AND HYPOTHESIS*

THE preceding account of science has led us to assert that science is an activity of discovery of the relationships which hold between elements which can be immediately apprehended in sensation or imagination. If we were to insist that only knowledge of such relationships can be called scientific knowledge, we should have to face the objection that we can never know then that *all* whales are mammals or that *all* conductors in which a current is flowing are surrounded by a magnetic field or that *all* bits of matter are composed of sub-atomic particles, charged and uncharged, which are organized into atoms and these in turn into molecules, since we do not have all the evidence required to transform these statements into literal statements of fact. They must be regarded as statements which can be "confirmed" but not established by immediate apprehension. For this reason they have been called "hypotheses" by some writers and "predictions" by others.

It is useful, however, to distinguish between generalizations and hypotheses. A clear distinction is given in a recent logic text: [4]

A generalization is an inductive conclusion that has the following characteristics: (*1*) It states that something is true about many or all of the members of a certain class . . . (*2*) The evidence for it consists of a number of facts about individual members of the class . . . (*3*) The facts are evidence for the generalization because they are *instances* of the generalization . . . A hypothesis, on the other hand, has the following characteristics: (*1*) It states that something is true about an individual, or a number of specific individuals; it states that something has happened, is happening, or will happen, or that some state of affairs has existed, exists, or will exist . . . (*2*) The evidence for it consists in a number of facts about *other* events or states of affairs . . . (*3*) The facts are evidence for the hypothesis because they are *explained* by the hypothesis . . .

To this we must add a definition of "explanation":

. . . To say that one statement explains another is to say that the first statement (with the help of a third) logically implies the second . . .

[4] M. C. Beardsley, *Practical Logic*, Prentice-Hall, 1950, pp. 216, 219.

I should prefer to replace the phrase "with the help of a third" by "with the help of at least one other statement," but otherwise this account of "generalization," "hypothesis," and "explanation" is adequate for our present purposes. It is obvious that the first example mentioned above is a generalization since the evidence for it consists of observed instances in which whales were or are mammals. The second is likewise a generalization, but the third is a hypothesis, since the evidence for it consists of statements about the observable behavior of certain gases, or of cathode rays, or of oil drops in an electric field, or of tracks in a cloud chamber, etc.

It is impossible to deny that hypotheses have been of great value in the progress of scientific discovery. It is also undeniable that in many instances the uncritical acceptance of a hypothesis has been a positive bar to scientific progress. The reason is simply this: that whenever a hypothesis explains a given phenomenon, it is always possible that some other hypothesis (or hypotheses) may explain it equally well or better. We cannot put complete trust in a hypothesis until we have shown that all other possible alternatives could not explain equally well a given set of phenomena, and we are usually not in a position to do this. It is also possible, as in the case of the quantum theory, that new phenomena may be discovered which cannot be explained by the "classical" hypotheses. The hypotheses must be discarded then as a universal tool of explanation.

The situation is not quite the same in the case of generalizations. In most cases well-attested generalizations are merely subsumed under wider generalizations with the progress of science, as Kepler's laws of motion were subsumed under Newton's laws of gravitating bodies and as Newton's laws themselves are subsumed (as special cases) under the laws of relativity mechanics. In such instances the old generalization becomes merely a special case of the new, unless, of course, the new generalization is founded on new facts which contradict the old generalization. The point is that statements which report faithfully the relationships actually observed to hold between sensory phenomena cannot be disproved by any subsequent discoveries, and generalizations founded on such statements are not abandoned because they have been shown to be false but because they are too restricted in scope to be of any use.

We may now state what appears to be an invariable law of scientific progress: that progress in science is always accompanied by an effort to replace hypotheses by generalizations. I shall give three instances, drawn from three different epochs in the history of science. There is, first of all, the fact that Greek medicine arose as a scientific discipline when it learned to renounce the early speculative hypotheses concerning the origin and nature of disease and constructed instead generalizations which described the actual course of the disease from its earliest to its final stages. One of the Hippocratic writers is himself aware of this improvement in method: [5]

All who, on attempting to speak or to write on medicine, have assumed for themselves a postulate as a basis for their discussion — heat, cold, moisture, dryness, or anything else that they may fancy — who narrow down the causal principle of diseases and of death among men, and make it the same in all cases, postulating one thing or two, all these obviously blunder in many points even of their statements . . . I have deemed that it [medicine] has no need of an empty postulate, as do insoluble mysteries . . . Medicine has long had all its means to hand, and has discovered both a principle and a method, through which the discoveries made during a long period are many and excellent, while full discovery

---

[5] Hippocrates, *Ancient Medicine*, I–II, tr. by W. H. S. Jones, Loeb Classical Library, Harvard.

will be made, if the inquirer be competent, conduct his researches with knowledge of the discoveries already made, and make them his starting-point.

This marks the beginning of what has been called the "rational spirit" in Greek medicine. Secondly, there is the improvement in physics inaugurated by Newton when he abandoned all attempts to explain the *cause* of terrestrial and celestial motion and contented himself with giving a universally applicable description of such motions. Newton's *intent*, if not literally his accomplishment, is expressed in his famous statement, "I do not fabricate hypotheses" (*hypotheses non fingo*). He *did* unfortunately introduce the hypotheses of an absolute space and an absolute time in order to explain certain phenomena, for example, the phenomenon of the spinning bucket of water, but these hypotheses in turn were shelved by Einstein in his special theory of relativity in constructing a purely descriptive theory of relative motion. As a third example we may mention the abandonment by Heisenberg and Bohr of the classical hypothesis of atomic models in favor of purely descriptive laws which govern the behavior of the "observables" of quantum mechanics. In every single case we must admit that hypotheses still remain in the new science, but the important fact is this: that the advance has occurred because of the discarding of hypotheses in favor of generalizations. The conclusion we draw is not that science *can* at any moment abandon all hypotheses, but that it would be willing to do so if it could be provided with adequate generalizations to take their place. We may express this by saying that the *aim* of science is the discovery of the most inclusive sort of generalizations of which, by definition, individual "atomic" facts are instances.

We must now amend our definition of science and assert that science is an activity which aims at the discovery of the relationships which hold between elements which can be immediately apprehended in sensation or imagination or the discovery of generalizations of which these immediately apprehended relationships are instances. We may wish to call the first sort of knowledge "intuitive" or "indubitable" knowledge and the second "probable" knowledge, to mark the distinction between the two, but it is hardly necessary for our present purpose to tackle the thorny problem of the exact relation between these two sorts of knowledge.

4. SCIENCE AND THE REAL

I n the preceding sections I have attempted to show: (1) that science is a discipline of immediacy, in the sense that the elements which serve as the terms of the relationships discovered are themselves apprehended by sense or imagination; (2) that it differs from art since the assertion of relationships or of generalizations, of which these relationships are instances, must involve judgment, and art does not; (3) that science differs from technology in that technology is done for the sake of some end lying beyond the activity itself, while science is done for the sake of the characteristic pleasure which accompanies the act of discovery and is therefore a kind of play. By the use of statement (1) we can now state more clearly the relations of science and metaphysics and therefore of scientific fact and "reality."

It is necessary at the outset to remove one possible misconception. It is often asserted that anyone is a philosopher and in particular a metaphysician if it can be shown that he has quite definite beliefs concerning that which is real or that which exists. These are often called his "metaphysical presuppositions." Now it ought to be clear that the mere possession of such beliefs does not make a man a metaphysician any more than the possession of a body makes him a biologist. He becomes a metaphysician only when he attempts a critical analysis of these beliefs, and he remains a meta-physician only so long as he continues this analysis. All individuals, including children, appear to have some beliefs concerning what is real and what is not. If we were to say of a scientist therefore that his scientific work is based on meta-physical presuppositions, this would not distinguish him from the child playing hide and seek who believes, rightly or wrongly, in the existence of his unseen playmate. If science is relevant to metaphysics, this must be true, not because the scientist makes certain metaphysical assumptions, but because he is able to tell us by his method what is real. We must now examine this latter alternative.

We must observe first of all that the *criterion* by means of which we determine whether a given object of thought is real or not cannot itself be established by scientific methods. If our criterion is: "To be real a thing must be sensed," then it is clear that this criterion cannot be established by any method of observation or experiment. Observation (and judgment) can determine whether a given entity is real or not *according to* this criterion, but it cannot test the truth of the criterion itself. We may rephrase this by saying that in so far as science is empirical, it is unable to determine the truth or falsity of any criterion of reality or existence.

We must now ask whether in the case of *every* criterion, whatever its origin, science is able to tell us whether a given entity is real or not according to that criterion. Let us take the more general and rather more plausible criterion: "An entity is real if and only if it has sensible effects." This criterion might be used to "prove" the existence of the other side of the moon or the existence of atomic and sub-atomic particles. If the entity is itself observed and if we are quite sure that the "sensible effects" are *its* effects, then we can apply our criterion, but we must observe that this presup-poses that we also have a criterion to determine when we have a cause-and-effect relationship between observable entities. If we apply this criterion to determining the existence of the visible sun, we will argue that the visible sun exists, not because we see it, but because it makes us warm or produces evaporation of water or produces chlorophyll in plants.

The serious difficulties arise when, as in the case of the other side of the moon and atomic particles, the entities are not themselves perceivable. How can we determine in this case that the other side of the moon exists or that electrons exist? Let us take the case of the moon first. Clearly we may proceed here as in any case of confirming or disconfirming a hypothesis. *If* the other side of the moon exists, then we should expect certain gravitational effects on the earth when we apply the laws of Newtonian mechanics to this case. These effects are actually observed. Therefore our hypothesis is confirmed. Moreover in this case the hypothesis that the other side of the moon does *not* exist can be disconfirmed, that is, *if* the other side of the moon did not exist and if we assume the truth of the laws of Newtonian mechanics, including the law of gravitation, then we should note certain gravitational effects which in fact do not occur. Such an argument is founded on the assumption that there is no other body in the neighborhood of the earth which could produce the effects actually observed, but the truth of this assumption can be tested by simple observation. It is not difficult to persuade ourselves therefore of the existence of the other side of the moon, since we can observe certain "effects" which would be inexplicable without that assumption. Our argument in fact has tended to show that if the other side of the moon did not exist, certain phenomena would not occur, and this is equivalent to the argument that since they do occur, the other side of the moon must exist.

These phenomena can then be regarded as the sensible effects of the other side of the moon.

It will be noted, however, that we have not used our criterion of existence in this demonstration, that is, we have not argued that the other side of the moon exists because certain phenomena are its sensible effects. Before such a causal relation between the moon and these terrestrial phenomena could be established it would be necessary to assume the *existence* of the other side of the moon, and it would be trivial then to deduce its existence from this assumption. Our criterion therefore is not applicable in this case because it presupposes that one has a means of determining that certain sensible phenomena are the *effects* of an unperceived entity, and it is not only impossible to establish an exact causal relationship between an unseen cause and a seen effect, but even if this were possible, we should need to assume for such a demonstration that the cause itself exists.

It is clear that the same difficulties attend the application of our criterion for determining the existence of the electron. If we are certain that blurs on a photographic plate are caused by impinging electrons, it seems a little silly to conclude from this that electrons exist. It might be objected that we do at least know that *something* exists to produce these blurs, and that we are asserting merely that this something exists. But this objection is of little value. We are all willing to admit that the blurs have some cause. What is required in the present argument, however, is a demonstration that they are caused by the action of "electrons" which, whatever their intrinsic character, have at least a definite charge and mass. The description of such a causal relation between an unperceivable cause and a perceivable effect cannot ordinarily be given in detail, and as we have seen, if we did know that it could be rigorously shown, it would be trivial then to conclude that the cause exists.

It is clear from the case of the moon that what we *do* use ordinarily to demonstrate the existence of unperceivable entities are the ordinary rules for the confirmation or disconfirmation of hypotheses. Thus we attempt to show that if the entity in question exists, then if we make certain other assumptions, which state usually that the entity in question obeys some familiar physical law, we are led to expect certain sensible "effects." We should like to show in addition that if the entity in question does not exist, then on the basis of these same assumptions we are led to expect that certain phenomena will not occur. If they do occur, we are in a position to assert conclusively that the entity does exist. In the case of the moon this second step is equivalent to the demonstration that there is no other body which by the laws of Newtonian mechanics could produce the observed sensible effects, and this proposition can be verified, as we have seen, by direct inspection of the heavens.

In the case of the electron the problem is much more complex. We tend to think of an electron as an entity confined to a limited region of space, with an invariable mass, size, shape and a well-defined velocity at any point in space or any instant in time. In short, we think of it as a particle, analogous apart from size to a grain of sand or a mote in a sunbeam. We may, of course, attempt to consider an electron merely as an unknown "X" which in some mysterious way "has" mass, position, velocity, etc., without attempting to visualize it, but it is obvious on reflection that whenever we do attempt to construct an imaginative or intuitive picture of it that the materials for this picture must be drawn from the familiar world of the senses. Electrons as terms of discourse may have properties quite different from the things of our ordinary experience, but as visualized or visualizable entities they become, so to speak, naturalized citizens of our familiar sense world.

There is a serious difficulty here since we do know, whatever the intrinsic character of electrons, that they do *not* behave like the objects of our everyday experience. A beam of electrons, for example, if directed on a thin sheet of metal foil, will form a diffraction pattern on a screen placed behind the foil, and it can easily be shown that this would never happen if the electrons were particles obeying the laws of our familiar macroscopic world. Furthermore if the electron changes its energy or momentum, such changes take place in a discontinuous fashion in a manner which satisfies certain "quantum conditions," and this is also unintelligible if applied to bodies in the observable world. The result is this: If by "electron" we mean "a visualizable entity which obeys the quantum conditions and behaves like an observable particle," then we are confronted with a simple contradiction, and to assert the existence of such entities is to assert the existence of entities which behave like observable particles and yet do not behave like them. We might attempt to escape this dilemma by asserting the existence of particles which resemble ordinary particles but do not behave like them, but aside from any formal difficulties here, the maintenance of this distinction demands a power of abstraction which few, if any, of us possess. Since our entities are assumed to be visualizable, we would be asked to *visualize* discontinuous changes of energy and momentum, and I must confess, for my part, that I have not been able to do so.

To assert the existence of an electron is quite a different sort of thing therefore from asserting the existence of the other side of the moon. We assert merely the existence of a non-visualizable somewhat with a limited set of properties such as mass and charge. It must also be remembered that such a proposition can merely be confirmed, that is, such a proposition appears as the antecedent in a hypothetical statement of the form: if a somewhat having such and such properties exists, then we should expect such and such observable results. If we do get these results, then our hypothesis has been confirmed. But it is well known that the same set of results will confirm two different hypotheses. This is not at all embarrassing if we regard hypotheses merely as devices for making accurate predictions or, to use Bohr's phrase, as statements of "complementary" aspects of physical reality. We then assert merely that a whole set of different hypotheses may be confirmed by the same (or similar) evidence. It is embarrassing, however, when we have, say, two propositions which assert that an entity exists and at the same time ascribe contrary properties to it. Thus I cannot assert that an entity exists which is *both* a system of waves and a particle, although I may legitimately consider separately the assertions "The electron is a system of waves" and "The electron is a particle." Each of these propositions may be confirmed without confirming the proposition, "The electron is both a system of waves and a particle."

The result may be expressed as follows: that which we call "the electron" cannot simultaneously have all the properties which we may plausibly assign to it on the basis of experimental evidence, nor can we be *quite* sure that it has any of them. This uncertainty springs from the fact that if we have two or more hypothetical accounts of the nature of the electron with relatively equal predictive power, we cannot be certain that one of these rather than another is the proper account of the electron, nor can we with any set of hypotheses be quite sure that there is not some hypothesis, as yet undreamed of, which is not more plausible than any previously advanced. The plausibility of a hypothesis depends on the accuracy of our methods of confirmation, and it is impossible

to set any practical bounds to the accuracy with which
physical observations may be made. (I am assuming here
that Heisenberg's "principle of indeterminacy" expresses a
theoretical bound for such accuracy.) Whenever new refine-
ments of observational technique are introduced, we shall
conceivably need new hypotheses to predict the new data.
The conclusion seems to be that it would be a little absurd for
us at any stage in the development of physics to assert that
we now have an adequate description of "physical reality."
It is almost equally misleading to assert that we have an
account which "corresponds" to physical reality, although
it is not a literal description, since we have no means of
judging the closeness of the correspondence.

The conclusion that we can draw from these remarks is
that it is absurd for physics (or any science) to consider that
its proper task is to give an account of the nature of physical
reality (or chemical reality or biological reality or mathematical reality), since if by some miracle it has been able to
do so, it can never know that it has, and if it has not and has
only an approximate account, it can never know the degree
of approximation or correspondence. It is for this reason
that the ideal of science will always be the construction of
descriptive generalizations rather than the elaboration of
hypothetical accounts of reality. Since science by its own
methods has no means of telling us what is real or establish-
ing criteria for reality, it ought to confine itself to its proper
task of describing, as completely and simply as possible, "the
relations between the manifold aspects of our experience." [6]

5. *SCIENCE AND MORALITY*

WE have observed in the preceding chapters that the artist is
never a moralist; nor is he on the other hand an immoralist.
He is, to coin a word, simply an "amoralist." He is in fact

[6] Niels Bohr, *Atomic Theory and the Description of Nature*, p. 18.

simply indifferent to matters of good and bad, right and wrong. It is for this reason that he is so often misunderstood in the way in which Tolstoy misunderstood de Maupassant, and is praised irrelevantly for the morality of his conclusions and criticized for the immorality of his themes.

Precisely the same remarks apply to the scientist. Science is dedicated neither to the improvement of mankind nor to its destruction, but merely to the discovery of truth. This indifference of the scientist to good and evil, to the practical consequences of his discoveries, often leads the moralist to regard him as an immoral monster, since he does not *care* what the consequences are. This is again an instance of polemic methodology, since if the scientist did care about these consequences, he would no longer be a scientist but a political administrator. We should not complain therefore of the neutralism of the scientist, but we may very well complain of the positive immorality of those who are in a position to control the political or economic consequences of the scientist's discoveries, and we may very well insist that the scientist, *as scientist*, is not qualified to determine how his discoveries shall be used.

This last statement will be disputed by all those who believe that "science can save us," politically as well as technologically. They will argue both that science is the only method that will provide us with the facts on which intelligent political action can be based and that science can also provide us with the directives concerning how these facts should be used. There are some extremists of this school who wish to assert apparently that only a knowledge of the facts is necessary for intelligent political action, but this position is too childish to deserve much attention. Scientific facts are themselves neutral, and assert merely that which is the case and never that which *ought* to be the case. We must consider much more seriously, however, the view that by using the *methods* of science we can also decide what ought to be the case.

It must be made clear, first of all, that we can agree with the proponents of this "science of man" that science is the only method by which the facts can be discovered on which intelligent political action can be based, and without logical contradiction *disagree* that science is able to tell us what to do about the political and physical situation revealed by science. If it is a question of fact, then science alone can answer such a question. Can science, however, answer the question: What should we do in the presence of such and such facts?

Those who answer "Yes" to this question present the following persuasive argument: All ethical and social principles which tell us what we ought to do in the presence of the facts must be tested and established in the same way that the facts themselves are established, that is, by the method of experiment. We must not blindly accept certain principles from tradition or religion or abstract philosophy; we must accept only those principles which have been tested by experience. We must consider such principles as hypotheses awaiting confirmation by experience. Those which prove to be satisfactory we retain; those which cannot be tested by experiment or which prove positively unsatisfactory, we discard. This is roughly the view which John Dewey, the philosophic patron saint of this movement, has preached so eloquently.

The real problem here is this: How does one discover that a given hypothesis is satisfactory? In natural science the test is simply: Do the conclusions which follow from the hypothesis state relations which can actually be observed? In other words, we argue that if the hypothesis were true, such and such ought to be the observable result (within certain arbitrary limits of experimental error). If we do get this result, we say that our hypothesis is confirmed; otherwise it is disconfirmed. The test then for a satisfactory scientific hypothesis is quite simple; it is simply the correspondence of prediction and observed fact.

What is the corresponding criterion for a satisfactory ethical hypothesis? It is certainly not the test previously mentioned: the correspondence of prediction and observed result. The importance of ethical principles is not that they enable us to predict what will happen but that they enable us to judge the value of what happens. We need, in other words, a criterion of the value of the results. If we have none, we can merely say: If such and such principles are put into practice, the results will be such and such. This is trivial, however, since we are interested, not in what results will follow the application of our principles, but whether such results are "good" or "bad."

In judging the adequacy of an ethical hypothesis by this method we must either apply arbitrary criteria to the results or insist that our criteria are "instinctive" or "obvious." It is important to note that in neither case are the *criteria* tested by the experiment. Thus I may assume that the results are good if they produce the maximum amount of pleasure for all concerned, but my criterion, which equates "good" with "that which produces pleasure," cannot be established by experiment. The criterion for the "good," like the criterion for the "real," cannot be established by scientific methods. All that an experiment can determine is whether our ethical hypothesis will lead to results which can be evaluated by our criteria. The criteria themselves are a priori in the sense that they are not established or disproved by the experiment. If one attempts to test *them* by experiment, they must in turn be judged by more ultimate criteria.

It is not my intention to deny all value to the procedure I have been criticising. The method of experiment is clearly a test which must be applied to all practical rules of conduct and all principles of legislation. It is necessary to discover the actual results to which they lead, but one evaluates the results by the use of certain criteria which lie beyond the reach of experiment. The examination of these criteria is the function of philosophy; their application to the results of social experiment is the task of science, or more properly, of social technology.

The conclusion to which we have been led in this chapter is that the aim of science is the most general description of the relations which hold within our experience; that it is not dedicated to the improvement of man nor the control of nature; and in particular that it is incapable of elucidating the meaning of certain terms, such as "real" and "good," which it is accustomed to apply to the terms or results of its observations. We must now turn to philosophy and examine the methods by which it claims to achieve a certain kind of insight forbidden to science.

[FIVE]

Philosophy

1. *PHILOSOPHY AND METHODOLOGY*

WE have observed in Chapter One that, corresponding to a philosophy of art, a philosophy of science, and a philosophy of religion, there should be a philosophy of philosophy which seeks to determine the limits and methods of philosophy itself. It is astonishing that this problem has received so little systematic attention from philosophers. Every philosopher *has* presumably his own conception of the nature of his discipline, and this he often states explicitly or implicitly, but it is usually stated as a dogma, and he will tolerate no criticism of it by himself or others. There are philosophers indeed who will passionately insist that philosophy is the science of criticism but will refuse to subject *that* principle to any criticism. One is invited to conclude that the average philosopher's conception of his discipline is an accident of birth, training, geography, or temperament, and in most cases it might be more accurate to conclude that he has no conception of the ends or methods of his chosen field. In the latter case Kant has given us a vivid description of the consequences: "Thereby it happens, that, since the philosophers themselves have failed to develop the idea of their science, the elaboration of it has no determined goal and no certain guiding principle, and philosophers, ignorant, by reason of their arbitrary decision on this point, of the way they ought to take and always quarreling among themselves con-

cerning the discoveries which each has claimed to make by
his own procedure, have made their science to be despised,
first by others, and finally indeed by themselves." [1] This is the
tragedy of contemporary philosophy that it is despised, not
merely by the scientist and poet, but secretly by the philosopher himself.

What reason shall we give for this refusal by the philosopher to develop or defend his conception of philosophy? His
refusal, I suggest, comes from his reluctance to get *outside*
philosophy and look at it from some other point of view, as
the scientist looks at science from the outside when he begins
to do philosophy of science. The philosopher seems to assume
that there *is* no outside to his discipline. This is equivalent to
assuming that methodology, for instance, is itself a part of
philosophy. According to this assumption he would be correct
in asserting that there could be no philosophy of philosophy,
as we have observed before, since one would be attempting
to apply the method of philosophy in order to determine the
method of philosophy, and he is quite aware of the absurdity
of this procedure. He asserts therefore some more or less
arbitrary dogma and contents himself with ridiculing the
alternative views of his colleagues.

The only solution to this difficulty seems to be to persuade the philosopher that he *can* get outside his discipline;
that the method of philosophy is only one among a set of
methods of coördinate disciplines; that in this outside realm,
which is the realm of methodology, one can operate by
unique procedures which are not identical with those in any
of the subordinate disciplines.

2. PHILOSOPHY AND MORAL CONCERN

KIERKEGAARD contrasted the philosophers of his time
with the great Greek philosophers by insisting that the mod-

---

[1] *Kritik der Reinen Vernunft*, B 872.

ern philosophers never point out the relevance of their conclusions to their own *Existenz* whereas this relevance and concern were always obvious in the Greeks. This is certainly true in the case of Socrates for whom every philosophical problem was *his* problem, who deduced philosophical conclusions in order that he might *act* on them. There is no divorce in Socrates between philosophical theory and moral practice and thus, as Kierkegaard pointed out, Socrates is never comic as every philosopher is who deduces world-shaking conclusions and forgets that he is part of the system. But this marriage of theory and practice is hardly less obvious, although less dramatic, in Heraclitus, Epicurus, Plato, and Aristotle. The philosophy of each can be regarded as an elaborate attempt to answer the question, posed as early as Pythagoras, "What kind of life should a man live?" and there is some evidence, at least, that each tried to make his own life conform to his theoretical answer.

Should we agree with Kierkegaard, however, that modern philosophy has renounced this point of view and has transformed philosophy into a purely theoretical discipline? If so, we might expect to find traces of this tendency in Descartes, the traditional founder of modern philosophy. It is true that Descartes seems to be activated merely by a passionate desire to discover truth, wherever it may be found. But we must still ask, What disposes him to select *these* problems for solution rather than others? Does he do metaphysics merely in order to provide a satisfactory foundation for his theoretical science? There is evidence to the contrary. The title page of the first edition of the MEDITATIONS reads: MEDITATIONS ON FIRST PHILOSOPHY IN WHICH THE EXISTENCE OF GOD AND THE IMMORTALITY OF THE SOUL ARE DEMONSTRATED. The second edition reads: MEDITATIONS ON FIRST PHILOSOPHY IN WHICH THE EXISTENCE OF GOD AND THE DISTINCTION OF THE HUMAN SOUL FROM THE BODY ARE DEMON-

STRATED. Clearly Descartes's initial interest here was practical or moral rather than theoretical.

In Kant the practical intent of metaphysics is re-established in his assertion that the three fundamental themes of metaphysics are: God, freedom of the will, and immortality. These are problems which no individual attempts to solve out of idle curiosity, although he may attempt to apply a favorite dialectical method to an analysis of the solutions which others have offered. Even if metaphysics be defined as that discipline which attempts to draw the proper distinction between reality and appearance, it is still true, as A. E. Taylor has pointed out,[2] that when we call an object "real" or a "reality," we wish to emphasize "that it is something of which we categorically *must* take account, whether we like it or not, if some purpose of our own is to get its fulfillment." In general the real is important because it is that of which account must be taken. One pursues metaphysics, if one pursues it at all, because one hopes to find an answer to the question "What am I and how am I related to the society and universe in which I find myself?"

One can find more recent definitions of philosophy which support this conception, for example: "Philosopy is an attempt to clarify those fundamental beliefs which finally determine the emphasis of attention that is the base of character."[3] It is not difficult to demonstrate that all philosophical conclusions have their practical consequences. All one needs to recognize then is that all philosophy, when it is done without constraint, is done for the sake of these conclusions and their intimate personal relevance. One does abstract epistemology, for example, in order to be quite sure that he is not being deceived about important

[2] *Elements of Metaphysics*, Methuen, 12th ed., 1946, p. 51.

[3] A. N. Whitehead, *Adventures of Ideas*, p. 125, quoted by John Dewey in *The Philosophy of Alfred North Whitehead*, Northwestern University Press, 1941, p. 658.

matters when he says he *knows* something about them. Socrates must still be our model philosopher, and it is not surprising that an age, which is on the whole indifferent to what he called "the state of one's soul," should also be indifferent to metaphysics and the theory of knowledge and ethics in the traditional sense and devote itself rather to logical and linguistic analysis of the statements of genuine philosophers. Even here one may often find a passionate conviction of the practical importance of not being taken in by traditional philosophy and religion and of confining one's self to statements that have "warranted assertibility." This is, however, almost the only point of similarity between this school of modern "philosophy" and philosophy of the Socratic type. Modern "philosophy," as we shall argue, in its attempt to ape the methods of science, has merely succeeded in driving genuine philosophy from the stage. It has failed to repudiate, as Socrates repudiated according to the PHAEDO, the method of science in favor of the proper dialectical method of philosophy.

3. *DIALECTIC*

W E have pointed out in a previous chapter that philosophy is not the only discipline that is founded on what we have called moral concern. It will hardly be disputed that the religious, i.e. the man of religion, is passionately dedicated to the salvation of his own soul or that of others. (In Christianity he is assured that he saves his *own* life by a devotion to the happiness of others.) In particular cases it is difficult to know when we should call a man a philosopher and when we should call him a religious. The last act of Socrates was to leave instructions for sacrificing a cock to the god Aesclepius. Is this the act of a philosopher? Can we be sure that Socrates, in one of his prolonged mystic trances, is philosophizing? Bertrand Russell [4] has said that philosophy is a blend of mysticism and science, and the paradoxical union of these two antithetical qualities in the philosopher is no more obvious than in the case of Socrates whose intellectual acuity was always tempered by a simple, stubborn piety.

But Socrates was more than pious and therefore he was more than a mere "believer." He was also a formidable dialectician, and without this capacity for dialectic we should not be entitled to call him a philosopher. The dialectic of Socrates, however, as well as the dialectic of Zeno of Elea, is logically indistinguishable from the method of *reductio ad absurdum* previously employed by the Pythagorean mathematicians: one disproves a statement, made perhaps by one's opponent, by showing that by purely logical methods one can deduce from it either the contradictory of the statement itself or the contradictory of some other statement which is considered true by one's opponent. The Pythagoreans used the method with a positive intent to show that if a given statement could be shown to be false, then its contradictory must be true. Socrates and Zeno used the method negatively as a method of disproving the statements of their opponents. Socrates could not have found a better instrument for disproving the "wisdom" of his contemporaries and justifying thereby the wisdom of the oracle.

It is important for our present purpose to note that Socrates did not invent the method he used; he merely invented a new way of using it by applying it not to mathematical subject matter but to the statements of his contemporaries concerning virtue, piety, knowledge, and justice. We have here a historical illustration of the fact that philosophical argument cannot differ in its logical form from the arguments used in science. No philosophical argument can appeal for its formal validity to principles that will not also

[4] *Mysticism and Logic*, Norton, 1929, p. 1.

be recognized by the mathematician and natural scientist. Thus philosophical dialectic is nothing *sui generis*, if we consider merely its logical form; if it differs from scientific dialectic, it must be because of the subject matter to which it is applied. If philosophy has its links with religion in the sense that it is founded on moral concern, it is also linked with science by the logical identity of its dialectic.

We have asserted in passing that without a capacity for dialectic Socrates could not be called a philosopher. This statement clearly needs to be defended. We often call a man a philosopher because he thinks about certain kinds of things or has certain kinds of opinions or because he "takes things philosophically." We call a poem such as Wordsworth's PRELUDE a philosophical poem although there is hardly a trace of argument in it. In the same spirit we are tempted to call a scientist or even a critic of metaphysics a metaphysician because we can demonstrate that he has certain metaphysical beliefs. But clearly if to hold metaphysical beliefs were enough in itself to make one a metaphysician, then each of us would be one, since we all have beliefs concerning what is real and unreal, what exists and does not exist. What is ordinarily called "the philosophical attitude" is actually the attitude recommended by a particular *school* of philosophers, namely, the Stoics. Philosophy is an activity, not an attitude. One does not become a philosopher by writing a poem on God, man, and nature; one becomes a particular sort of poet. One can use philosophic themes in literature or painting without becoming a philosopher. Thus one cannot call Wordsworth or Goethe or Dante or Aeschylus or Lucretius a philosopher. Each of them is a poet, expressing certain intuitions and insights that we usually find only in genuine philosophy. In fact, in most philosophical poetry the philosophy is derivative, the echo of philosophic insights elaborated by genuine philosophers. Lucretius, if he, rather than Epicurus, had been responsible for the content of his poem as well as the language and form, would have to be considered a philosopher. As it is, he is a poet, and, I hasten to add, a very great one.

I do not wish to imply that it is impossible for the same man to be both an artist and a philosopher or for the same literary object to be both artistic and philosophic. Plato's PHAEDO is both a philosophic document and a great work of art. It is a philosophical document, however, not because its theme is the immortality of the soul, otherwise Wordsworth's famous ode would also be philosophic, but because it contains argumentative discourse concerning immortality. These arguments alone interest the genuine philosopher; for the dramatist who reads the dialogue they are barely distinguishable from the *mise en scène*. Hume's DIALOGUES ON NATURAL RELIGION is another example of a genuine philosophical document which, by reason principally of the style, is also a literary masterpiece. Santayana and Bertrand Russell in our own time have combined, perhaps less successfully, philosophic and artistic elements in their writing. The union of these two, often antagonistic, elements is not impossible; I have merely wished to emphasize that it cannot occur unless there is *some* dialectic present. Dialectic is not *enough* to make it philosophy, otherwise EUCLID would be philosophy, but it is *necessary*.

4. *ABSOLUTE PRESUPPOSITIONS*

PHILOSOPHY therefore shares with science, and more particularly with the abstract sciences of mathematics and logic, a concern for argument, and it is this dialectical element which appears so forbidding and alien to the artist and the religious. "Do not all charms fly at the mere touch of cold philosophy?" This is the theme of Keats' LAMIA. It is quite true that philosophy persists in its task of coolly deducing the consequences, of revealing contradictions, of making coherent what is initially incoherent, of bringing logical order into what is disorderly, and art and religion can never forgive its ruthlessness.

We must now consider those aspects of philosophical dialectic which seem strange and forbidding to the scientist. We shall consider first the views of the partisans of abstract science, that is, of pure mathematics and logic. The mathematician considers that it is his business to show that from certain assumptions one can derive certain (unexpected) consequences or theorems. When he has listed all his assumptions and carefully checked his inferences, he considers that he has a rigorous proof. When the proof (for a complicated proposition) is relatively short, it is also elegant. He is interested therefore in the number of his inferences and in the rigor (and often elegance) of his proofs, but in nothing else. It is maddening therefore when the philosopher asks him, "Are your assumptions true?" or "Are you sure you have listed *all* your presuppositions?" The mathematician is angry, first of all, because he is indifferent to the truth of his premises and secondly, because he knows (and quite rightly) that he has no means of demonstrating the truth of his premises. He is annoyed that the philosopher fails to appreciate the importance of his demonstration that if they *were* accepted as true, then all the consequences would also have to be regarded as true. And to suggest, as the philosopher does, that he has not stated all his presuppositions, is to suggest that his proof is not rigorous.

The philosopher and the natural scientist have often been in the wrong on these points. Good mathematics is not good by virtue of the truth of its premises but because of the soundness of its arguments. We may say, if we wish, that mathematics is merely dialectic, if by dialectic we mean sound argument. The philosopher therefore, although he respects dialectic, seems to demand more than dialectic, and at this point he parts company with the mathematician. We have said, in fact, that the philosopher is interested in deducing conclusions which have some bearing on questions in which he is morally concerned. He will not be satisfied therefore with some simple (or complicated) "if . . . then . . ." argument. He will want to know whether he ought to accept the premises. If he must and if the argument is sound, he can also accept the conclusions. Pure dialectic is, of course, a kind of play, but the philosopher is serious and will always repudiate mere logical virtuosity.

We might express this distinction by saying that the philosopher is interested, not in suppositions, but in presuppositions, if by "suppositions" we mean "assumptions he might make" and if by "presuppositions" we mean "assumptions he must make." It may make for clarity, however, to adopt Collingwood's terminology [5] and speak of "absolute presuppositions" when we wish to refer to assumptions that we must make, or, what comes to the same thing, assumptions that we invariably do make. I do not wish to concur, however, with Collingwood's definition of metaphysics as "the attempt to find out what absolute presuppositions have been made by this or that person or group of persons, on this or that occasion or group of occasions, in the course of this or that piece of thinking." [6] The metaphysician, or more generally, the philosopher, is not interested in determining what absolute presuppositions have been held by someone else. If he were, he would merely have determined that such and such is or was the case. He would then be doing merely

[5] R. G. Collingwood, *An Essay on Metaphysics*, Oxford, 1940, chap. V.
[6] *Ibid.*, p. 47.

that sort of science which we call history, or more particularly, history of ideas. The philosopher wants to find out
what *he* believes, not for the sake of scientific introspection,
but because he is aware that these beliefs have important
consequences for his own happiness and perfection. He needs
something, in short, on which he may *build*, and although the
building proceeds by the methods of logical dialectic, logic
itself cannot provide him with the foundations. It is in this
sense that Descartes's procedure will always be the model for
philosophy, although one need not concur with Descartes's
own "absolute presuppositions." It is also in this spirit that
Plato distinguishes mathematics and (philosophical) dialectic: [7] the former is bound to hypotheses, the latter rises
above hypotheses.

Philosophy then is the search for absolute presuppositions, but we must not regard these presuppositions as form-
ing an eternal, non-human realm of absolute truth. These
presuppositions are human, perhaps all too human, and may
vary from individual to individual and from epoch to epoch.
Philosophic truth therefore is quite a different sort of thing
from scientific truth. Whereas scientific truth is universal and
impersonal, philosophic truth is always intensely personal.
The common complaint that philosophers do not agree is
therefore stupid and irrelevant; what is astonishing is that
there should be any agreement. It is, of course, equally absurd to argue, as Kant did, that philosophers must agree on
their fundamental presuppositions. Whether there is agreement or not must be discovered; it cannot be presupposed.
What certainly does vary from individual to individual is the
capacity to ferret out these presuppositions, and this facility
and honesty in self-examination is the characteristic which
distinguishes the philosophic genius from the bungler.

[7] *Republic*, 511 B.

5. PHILOSOPHY AS TRANSCENDENTAL

THE philosopher's complaint about dialectic, as we have seen, is that it gets us nowhere. It confines us to the realm of uninterpreted symbols, to the realm of merely logical truth. The criticism of the natural (empirical) scientist is almost identical with that of the philosopher. He wants to use mathematics and logic as tools to help him in his exploration of the physical world. He wants to find some interpretation of the abstract symbols of mathematics which will enable him to assert that his premises are true (or at least probable) and that he may therefore expect that the consequences of these premises, as logically deduced from the latter, are also true or probable. Pure mathematics, with its self-contained logical beauty, seems to him as useless and trivial as it does to the philosopher.

The resemblance ends at this point, however, since the *kind* of truth which the natural scientist demands of his "mathematical" premises is quite different from the kind which the philosopher demands. The philosopher is content if he "sees" intuitively that his premises are true; the natural scientist must see literally, by the use of his senses or imagination, that his premises are true (or probable). This is the distinction which we have previously expressed by saying that philosophy is a transcendental discipline, while science is a discipline of immediacy. This is a distinction of fundamental importance and requires careful attention.

A discipline of immediacy, we have said, necessarily makes some appeal to the senses or imagination in the course of pursuing its own end. In the case of science we have a discipline which attempts to discover certain relationships which hold between elements which are themselves given in sensation or imagination. It will sometimes be objected that such an account does not apply to pure mathematics since points or the number two are not given either in sensation or imagination. It will be discovered, however, that if one analyzes what one does when he gives a *proof* (say by the use of Peano's postulates and definitions) that $2 + 2 = 4$, he will discover that he merely uses certain rules, which tell him how he may manipulate the symbols "2," "$+$," "$=$," and "4," and certain logical principles, and by these rules of manipulation and these principles he derives the conclusion "$2 + 2 = 4$." Nor is the procedure essentially different when he gives a proof, ordinarily more complicated, that every algebraic equation with complex coefficients has a complex root. One tends to forget that in order to do mathematics one must have writing materials — a piece of paper, a blackboard, a smooth stretch of sand. The entities talked about in mathematics are not certain transcendental ideals, as the Greeks thought. They are certain marks or signs which *need* refer to nothing else. Mathematics is constituted, therefore, by the set of sentences which contain these marks or signs, and one is a mathematician by virtue of his ability to manipulate these signs and discover the relations which exist between the sentences which contain them. It is for this reason that one has recourse to writing materials. With sufficient powers of imagination and memory one could dispense with these crutches, but it would still be true that mathematics must appeal either to sense *or* imagination.

It is hardly necessary to defend our classification of empirical or natural science as a discipline of immediacy, since by calling it "empirical" we intend to draw attention to the fact that we must begin with relations between terms that are actually observed. The relations between the terms, for example, the causal relation, may not themselves be observable, but the entities talked about must be. The argu-

ments presented in the preceding chapter need not be repeated here.

The situation in the case of philosophy is quite different.
Here assertions are made involving terms and relations, none
of which is identifiable in sensation or imagination. Suppose
we examine the statement of Parmenides: "That which is
not, does not exist." Here that-which-is-not cannot be
identified in sensation or imagination, not because "to be"
means "to be identifiable in sensation or imagination," but
for the same reason that that-which-is cannot be identified
in sensation or imagination. Being and non-being can only
be thought; they cannot be sensed or imagined. For the same
reason, that-which-exists can only be thought. It might
seem less abstract to assert, "The void does not exist," but
then we should merely fail to see, as Parmenides saw quite
clearly, that the void is identical with non-being. In order to
avoid all possibility of asserting a logical tautology, we might
have taken another proposition of Parmenides, "Being cannot arise from non-being," the foundation of all subsequent
"laws of sufficient reason." If anyone assents to this proposition, and I fail to see how anyone can refuse his assent once
he has understood the meaning of the terms of the statement,
he is asserting the truth of a proposition in which the terms,
and the relation asserted to hold between them, cannot be
clarified by experience. "To arise from" means in this case
"to be produced or caused by," and Hume demonstrated
quite conclusively that this relation could never be discovered in sensation or imagination.

What shall we do with statements of this sort and with
the similar conclusions of Plato in the SOPHIST that being
participates both in sameness and otherness but that sameness and otherness do not participate in each other? [8] Shall
we dismiss them as mere nonsense or as simple verbal

[8] 255 E–257 A.

tautologies? To do so without examining their claim to some
sort of significance is to commit the worst errors of polemic
methodology. To do so on these grounds is to insist that the
whole of metaphysics, of which these are beautifully clear
examples, is mere nonsense.

I prefer to maintain a more tolerant attitude and agree
with Plato in his arguments in the THEAETETUS [9] and SOPH-
IST [10] that there are certain comparisons between the data
presented by the senses which are made as judgments only
by the mind itself; that in making such judgments the mind
itself introduces (or identifies) such terms or relations as
Being, Difference, Sameness, Change, Rest. Plato calls these
"the greatest kinds." These terms cannot be identified by
the senses if only by reason of the fact that they appear in
judgments *about* sense contents, and the senses make no
judgments. It is for this reason that mere perception is not
knowledge; knowledge always involves that sort of mental
decision which we call "judgment." The conclusion is that
the objects of sensation and imagination are not the only
objects of consciousness. There are also objects of thought,
and the discrimination and comparison of these is the task of
philosophy.

If we call such objects of thought "transcendental,"
merely to indicate that they are not empirical, that is, are
not given in sense or imagination, then we have a ready
means of distinguishing the judgments of science from the
judgments of philosophy. The judgments of science are
immediate in the sense that the terms talked about, although
not necessarily the relations asserted by the judgment to
hold between the terms, are empirical, whereas the judgments of philosophy are transcendental in the sense that the
terms talked about and the relations asserted to hold between

[9] 184 B–185 E.
[10] 254 D–255 E.

them are objects of thought and cannot be identified or clarified by an appeal to experience. With this distinction philosophy runs no risk of being confused with, or absorbed by, science. The one is a discipline of immediacy, the other a transcendental discipline.

6. *THE A PRIORI*

IN the preceding section we have been considering the objects of philosophic knowledge, or more precisely, the objects concerning which we have such knowledge, and we have contrasted these terms, which we have called objects of thought, with the terms concerning which we have scientific knowledge. We must now return to the previous statement that philosophy is the search for absolute presuppositions.

If we put these two statements together, it follows that philosophic knowledge can exist only as explicit awareness of some absolute presupposition, and this presupposition itself is an assertion that certain transcendental terms of thought have relations or predicates which are also transcendental. Knowledge of relationships which hold between transcendental objects clearly cannot be established by an appeal to sensation or imagination and, what is equally important, such knowledge cannot be discredited by such an appeal. It would follow that no scientific knowledge is capable of corroborating or disproving philosophic knowledge, if the latter does exist. Philosophic knowledge is simply knowledge of the absolute presuppositions of all our thinking, including scientific knowledge, and philosophy is the search for such presuppositions.

It is customary to say that experience is the origin of all scientific knowledge in the sense that we would not know what we were talking about in science without experience, i.e. sense experience, of these objects. Likewise we would not know that such and such relations actually held between such objects without some appeal to experience. It is usually regarded as a defect of philosophic knowledge that it cannot give such a short account of its origin. Empiricists in fact have always denied that transcendental objects of thought exist and have attempted to assimilate the method of philosophy to the method of empirical science. The result has been to insist that *all* knowledge must be scientific, in our sense of the term. David Hume is the most thorough and consistent representative of this movement, but I am assuming that the conclusions to which he was led are nothing but a *reductio ad absurdum* of the whole position.

It is possible, however, if we recur to our previous statements, to give an account of the origin of philosophic knowledge which is just as short as the statement of the empiricist that experience is the source of all knowledge. This account is simply: thought is the origin of all philosophic knowledge. The primary characteristic of thought which distinguishes it from sensation and imagination is that it always involves an act of judgment, but we wish to emphasize also in this case that thought has its own objects which can never be apprehended merely by sense or imagination. It is by thinking therefore that one becomes aware of these transcendental objects of thought and of the equally transcendental relations which hold between them. To be aware of these objects and the relationships which hold between them is to be aware of the absolute presuppositions which philosophy aims to discover. "But isn't there some other control over philosophic thinking?" we shall ask incredulously. "Isn't there some sense in which it must be tested by experience?" The answer is: only by the experience of thinking consistently and resolutely, but never by sense experience or imagination or action. Plato's definition of thinking as the "mind's conversation with itself" emphasizes precisely the right points. Philosophic thinking is the mind's conversation with itself and with nothing outside itself. No sense experience could confirm or disconfirm its conclusions. It is thrown back on its own native resources.

The ordinary criticism of this position by pragmatists and empiricists is that if philosophic knowledge is to be attained merely by an act of rational intuition, then the philosopher is entitled to believe anything he pleases, even the most extravagant fantasies. This criticism, however, begs the question, since it assumes that if there is no external control over philosophic thinking, then such thinking, even when it faithfully pursues its own method, must fall into error. It must be made clear that the philosopher is never entitled to establish by thought that which can be confirmed or disconfirmed by experiment. An intuition that the earth is flat is, therefore, not a philosophic intuition; it is merely bad science. The critics of this position, therefore, ought to be quite sure that they are attacking the theory itself and not some caricature of it.

Secondly, it will be necessary for them to re-examine their conviction that there is a necessity in experimental knowledge which is lacking in philosophic knowledge. If I ask, "Why must I believe that flame produces heat?" the answer is, "Because I *feel* the heat when the flame appears." There is no more ultimate reason. If I likewise ask, "Why must I believe that nothing happens without a cause?" the answer is: "Because I *see* that this is so." The intuition in the second case is not sensory or imaginative, but it does not follow for this reason that it does not exist nor that I should not feel it to be just as necessary as the most stubborn empirical awareness. Flame causes heat because I find in the presence of both that I cannot believe otherwise. Likewise, what does not exist cannot give rise to anything that does, because I cannot think otherwise. There is, in short, a necessity in philosophic thinking which one is tempted to call "subjective" since it is discovered simply when one begins to think philosophically, but since it is just as independent of our wishes and desires as empirical knowledge, it might equally well be called "objective." One cannot believe what one wishes in philosophy but only what one *sees* intuitively after vigorous and prolonged meditation.

It is customary to call concepts which are not derived from sense experience a priori concepts and knowledge which is not dependent on sense experience a priori knowledge. It would follow then that the transcendental objects of thought of which we have been speaking can be called a priori concepts and likewise that all philosophic knowledge is a priori knowledge. There is a further consequence, however, of equal importance: Only philosophic knowledge is a priori. All scientific knowledge, since it is knowledge of the relations of elements presented immediately in sensation or imagination, is a posteriori. This is obviously true for all empirical scientific knowledge, the knowledge pursued by natural science. It is also true of mathematical knowledge, as we have seen, and also of the knowledge attained by mathematical logic. It is therefore possible for us to concur completely with the statement of C. I. Lewis that "philosophy is the study of the a priori"[11] —but for quite different reasons. In particular we need not distinguish between analytic a priori knowledge and synthetic a priori knowledge, a distinction which has become traditional since Kant. Kant considered "All bodies are extended" to be analytic since the meaning of the predicate was contained in the meaning of the subject term. Other definitions of analytic propositions have been given: that they are true by definition, or by reason of synonymy, or because they are "logically true." Re-

[11] *Mind and the World-order*, Scribner's, 1929, p. 24.

cent criticism of this distinction[12] between analytic and
synthetic propositions has tended to show, however, that no
sharp distinction between the two can be made. We shall at
any rate refuse to make this distinction which would relegate
mathematics to the domain of analytic a priori knowledge
and shall insist instead that the proper distinction is between
a priori knowledge, represented by philosophy, and a posteriori knowledge represented by science. All a posteriori
knowledge is necessary because it is apprehended by an
act of sensation or imagination, or more accurately, by an
act of judgment founded on sensation or imagination; a
priori knowledge is necessary because it is apprehended by
an act of judgment which is directed merely to certain objects of thought.

7. OBJECTIONS AND ALTERNATIVES

THE account of philosophy given in this chapter would not
be accepted, I am sure, by the majority of contemporary
philosophers. I should like to believe, however, that Socrates,
Plato, Descartes, and Kant, to mention no lesser names,
would each find something congenial in this conception,
and I should be quite content if I were sure that the definition of "philosophy" we have been constructing would not
seem wholly implausible to any member of this group. I am
aware, at any rate, of my positive indebtedness to each.

Contemporary philosophy commonly distinguishes two
types of philosophy: speculative philosophy and analytic
philosophy, as if these were two species of the genus, philosophy. They are actually two incompatible conceptions of
philosophy. It is notorious, in fact, that the practitioners
of one type will have nothing to do with the other. The

[12] Cf. W. V. Quine, "Two Dogmas of Empiricism," *The Philosophical
Review*, LX, 1, Jan. 1951, pp. 20–43.

method of philosophy must be *either* speculation or analysis or something else of the sort I have suggested.

Bergson and Whitehead may be taken as representatives of speculative philosophy. The aim of philosophy, according to each, is the construction of an adequate cosmology, which shall include certain elements that have been traditionally subsumed under metaphysics, epistemology, and ontology. If physics be taken in its older sense as an account of the nature of the universe, then the aim of philosophy is the construction of a completely adequate physics. In Whitehead's words, "Speculative Philosophy is the endeavor to frame a coherent, logical, necessary system of general ideas in terms of which every element of our experience can be interpreted." [13] The historical model for this sort of philosophy is Plato's TIMAEUS, and just as Plato insisted that the TIMAEUS must be considered merely a "likely story" and not dogmatic science, so the contemporary practitioners of cosmology consider merely that they have a hypothesis concerning the nature of things which is more accurate than the implicit cosmologies of contemporary and classical science. They are quite willing to admit, however, that what they have is merely a hypothesis.

Now it is the defect of the method of hypothesis, as we have often noted, that, whatever hypothesis may be recommended, some other incompatible hypothesis may be just as successful in interpreting the phenomena which need to be explained, and furthermore with the discovery of new phenomena our hypothesis may need to be abandoned over night, if it is merely an arbitrary device used for purposes of explanation. Plato's description of the physical universe is now ridiculous if taken as a literal account of the nature of things, and Bergson's remarks on biology and Whitehead's on quantum physics are already dated. They possess, of course,

[13] A. N. Whitehead, *Process and Reality*, Macmillan, 1929, p. 4.

genuine historical value as the efforts of competent minds to frame a cosmology which shall be adequate to the science of their times, but in so far as they are merely arbitrary, speculative hypotheses they possess nothing to warrant the enduring attention of philosophers.

If they possess anything of value in them, and I would certainly insist that they do, it is by virtue of that in them which is *not* arbitrary, not merely speculative, that which by contrast we might call "necessary." Whitehead's admiration of Plato's remarks on the nature of space might be put in this form: that this is the way in which space *has* to be thought about, although Whitehead, I am sure, would not have approved of this mode of expression. Similarly Bergson's analysis of motion and the relation of concepts to duration will be valuable long after the vagaries of his positive cosmology have been forgotten and neglected. What is valuable in so-called speculative philosophy are those insights which are *not* mere speculation but the result of intense philosophic thinking of the sort we have previously described. That they are used for their "explanatory" value need not deceive us, since they are used, not because they promise to be successful, but because we have discovered that they *must* be used.

Speculative philosophy then, in so far as it is philosophy, is not speculative, and in so far as it is speculative, is not philosophy but bad science, which will be relegated to the scientific scrap heap as all such theories are. Similar remarks apply, not merely to cosmology, but to all systems of metaphysics, ontology, epistemology, and normative ethics. If the insights on which they are constructed have no intrinsic intelligibility or necessity, then they must be dismissed as worthless superstitions, incapable of empirical verification, which provide empty exercises in dialectic for minds incapable of genuine philosophy or science.

The approach of analytical philosophy, by contrast, is

direct, not hypothetical. It wishes to discover the meanings of certain words and sentences which occur in philosophy or science or in ordinary speech. The aim of philosophy accordingly is to clarify meanings, and some philosophers have asserted that philosophy is merely this activity of clarification and that it ends with no genuine pronouncements of its own. Thus one might wish to clarify the meaning of such words as "good," "right," "real," "is," or even "the" and "a," and for this work of clarification one is entitled to use all the help which can be offered by linguistics, semantics, and logic.

Now it must be admitted that *part* of the activity of philosophy is just this work of clarification of meaning. Unless one is quite clear about the meanings of "is not" and "is," he cannot agree (or disagree) with Parmenides' statement that "What is can never arise from what is not." It does not follow, however, that philosophy is entitled to usurp the function of clarifying the meaning of *all* words used in science or ordinary speech. Is philosophy entitled to clarify the meaning of "business" in the sentence "Business is business" or the meaning of "linear independence" in algebra? The meaning of "linear independence" is clarified by analysis of how algebraists use it, on what occasions and in what contexts, and the same may be said, *mutatis mutandis*, of "business." It is characteristic of such words and phrases that they are clarified either by a study of their common usage or by an act of sensation (and a correlative act of pointing) or both. Thus one can clarify the meaning of the word "red" by a formal study of the linguistic contexts in which the word is commonly used or by an appeal to a certain sensory or imaginative content. Hume called this latter procedure the method of clarifying ideas by referring to the impressions from which they arose. By referring to common usage or to sensory impressions one can clarify the meanings of most of the words used in science or ordinary speech, but this is certainly not true of the words peculiar to philosophy. As a philosopher one does not attempt to discover the meaning of the word "good" by studying the way in which the word has been used or is used by one's contemporaries nor is there any possible sense experience that one can refer to which will be enlightening without some *prior* agreement that such and such an experience is good. In short philosophy is the activity of clarifying, not the meaning of all words, but only of some words. Its method of clarification is by thinking and not by appeal to usage or sensation or imagination.

There is an objection to this notion of clarification by thinking which will be offered by the partisans of the sociology of knowledge. It will be said that, although I do not explicitly refer to common usage in attempting to discover the meaning of philosophic words, the meaning they have for me is still determined by common usage in the sense that it is the way I have been taught to use the word which constitutes its meaning for me. Thus in attempting to make clear the meaning of the word "exist" I am merely making explicit a meaning which has been "drummed into me" by my teachers and society. Philosophic thought would then be no independent act of legislation or discovery but a mere echo of common usage.

The difficulty in such a view is this: Let us admit that the meaning of all these primitive philosophic words is imposed on each individual by society. We must now ask: How do they acquire this meaning for society? It is hardly satisfactory to say that the meanings have been acquired from a *previous* society, since this merely postpones the difficulty. Nor can one say that they are simple conventions which have proven to be pragmatically useful, since in so far as their meaning is genuinely conventional it is by definition unaffected by any practical applications, and if it is meant that such words initially have vague and uncertain meanings which are fixed and determined by practice, then we must remember, what the logical empiricists have rightly pointed out, that sentences containing philosophic (metaphysical) words can never be confirmed or disconfirmed by experience and that therefore no experiment or empirical action will aid in fixing the meaning of such words. The partisans of the sociology of knowledge must then give us a hypothetical account of how the *first* society or the *first* man determined the meanings of the words he used, and it must explain how words such as "cause" and "exist," which cannot be clarified by sensation, came to be introduced into the language.

The conclusion would seem to be that no strictly empirical account of the origin of philosophic concepts can be given since such concepts originate in acts of judgment which are admittedly *about* empirical contents but which introduce terms and relations which the mind thinks "by itself." In this sense Kant's words on the first page of the CRITIQUE OF PURE REASON are still true: "There can be no doubt that all our knowledge begins with experience. . . . But . . . it does not follow that it all arises out of experience." [14] The historical confusion on this point has arisen because it has been assumed that because philosophic concepts arise only in the act of judgment about elements delivered by sensation or imagination that the concepts themselves were given by sensation or imagination. One needs to remember merely the traditional statement: "The senses make no judgments" to see the absurdity of this position. Some apparatus other than the senses, let us say "the mind," is required for the act of judgment. For this reason we can say that all relations between sense contents are discriminated by (or supplied by) the mind. If we call judgments

[14] *Critique of Pure Reason*, tr. by N. K. Smith, Macmillan, 1929, p. 41.

about sensory objects "empirical judgments," then it is true that all concepts arise from empirical judgments, and in this sense they have an "empirical origin." It must not be assumed, however, that they arise simply from sensation nor that practice will confirm their usefulness, if by practice we mean merely repeated sensation. What is important is the fact that they appear only in acts of *judgment* and not in acts of mere sensation, and they must be clarified therefore by thought and not sensation.

On the basis of the previous discussion it seems possible, therefore, to maintain the distinction between the philosophical clarification of concepts and empirical or linguistic methods, and we can refuse to assent to the view that philosophy is the activity of clarifying the meaning of all words which appear in scientific or ordinary discourse. (It might still be true that the method of philosophy must be used to clarify the meaning of words used to express the principles introduced to *justify* the methods of empirical or linguistic or logical clarification.) We must further object, however, that the end of philosophy is not merely to elucidate meanings, even if we restrict ourselves to the philosophic words. Philosophy, we have insisted, is not content until it has attained certain beliefs or judgments, what we may call "foundational statements," and those of course always contain philosophic concepts. Such statements may be merely definitions of certain philosophic words or they may be statements of the relations which hold between philosophic concepts. These are what we have called "absolute presuppositions." Analytic philosophy, with its attention fixed on clarification, has neglected this essential aspect of philosophy. It must be admitted that the *first* step in philosophy is the activity of clarification of meanings, but this is worthless to the philosopher if it does not lead him to the point where he can make an assertion. Philosophy, we have said, is an activity which involves judgment, in the sense that it aims always at the discovery of absolute presuppositions which it can then accept as foundational judgments, those which it feels *must* be true. Analysis, even when its practitioners have accepted the validity of intuition, has been reluctant to assert that certain statements are intuitively true, presumably because it might be contended that all such statements were analytic. With the discovery of the difficulty of distinguishing sharply between analytic and synthetic judgments, it should be easier to see that the important distinction is between a priori and a posteriori knowledge and that not merely are there certain concepts whose meaning is given intuitively but that also there is intuitive and a priori knowledge of the relations which hold between such concepts. Such knowledge is exactly that which we have called philosophic knowledge and is readily distinguishable from the knowledge by acquaintance which we have in art, the empirical knowledge which we have in science, and the kind of "knowledge" characteristic of religion.

[SIX]

Religion

1. THE USE OF RELIGION

THERE is a curious error in methodology which attends most discussions of religion. It is assumed, by reason of the fact that religion discourses of the Ultimate, the Highest, the Supreme, that religion itself is the highest and noblest activity of man. Consider the following passage: "And this shows that above and beyond our rational being lies hidden the ultimate and highest part of our nature, which can find no satisfaction in the mere allaying of the needs of our sensuous, psychical, or intellectual impulses or cravings." [1] The fact is that, from the standpoint of an objective methodology, religion is simply one fundamental type of human activity, coördinate with art, science, and philosophy, and only by resorting to polemic methodology can one insist that it is "better" or "higher" than any other discipline. The passage we have quoted ought to read: ". . . in addition to our rational nature, we possess a religious nature. . . ." Any determination of the proper function or use of religion must belong to methodology or, as we shall see in the following chapter, to that discipline which we may call inclusively "education."

[1] Rudolph Otto, *The Idea of the Holy*, tr. by J. W. Harvey, Oxford, 1926, p. 36. I have made numerous references to this book in writing this chapter since I discovered quite recently that it contained a gratifying confirmation of many of my own opinions and prejudices, and I have not hesitated to make use of whatever authority it may possess.

It must be admitted that it is difficult to maintain toward religion the strict objectivity demanded by objective methodology. We tend to take toward religion the attitude of reverence which is characteristic of the religious attitude itself. We tend to forget that just as philosophy of science is not science, so philosophy of religion is not religion. This is particularly true of the criticism of the traditional proofs for the existence of God. If such proofs are sound, it is by virtue solely of the logical structure of the argument, and this logical structure must be criticized by the same canons that apply to an argument concerning the distribution of the prime numbers. There is no "divine" logic which applies specifically to arguments concerning the existence or properties of the divine. Confusion on this point is responsible perhaps for the fact that until comparatively recent times philosophers have been unaware of the logical fallacies in some of the traditional proofs.[2]

It is important to remember furthermore that from the standpoint of what we may call "ordinary morality" the record of religion is not irreproachable. Moral atrocities have been committed in the name of religion, and such excesses are not characteristic merely of what are often called "primitive" religions. From the point of view of scientism, religion is not the highest of human activities but the lowest, since its statements have no "warranted assertibility" and are therefore merely an organized bundle of superstitions. The philosopher is apt to be merely contemptuous rather than openly antagonistic and asks with hastily veiled sarcasm how the theologian can be so uncritical of his primitive assumptions. But we are reminded again that all such attempts to degrade religion are instances of what we have called polemic methodology and that judgments about

[2] I have examined the logical structure of one of the classical proofs in "The Formal Fallacy of the Cosmological Argument," *The Journal of Religion*, XXIV, 3, July 1944, pp. 155–61.

the value of religion cannot be made either from the standpoint of religion or from that of any other discipline. We
must get outside religion and every other specialized discipline in order to discover the use of it.

The argument of the preceding chapters has tended to re-
enforce the following statements: (1) that religion is a practical discipline, that is, one does religion for the sake of an
ultimate moral perfection of the self; (2) that the means to
this perfection is the acquisition of a certain *disposition* of the
will and feelings, a disposition which we may characterize as
a passionate desire for virtue or "happiness"; (3) that the
methods which religion uses to awaken and sustain this
disposition or desire are rhetorical rather than logical. If it
can be shown that such measures are necessary in order that
virtue or moral perfection can be attained, we shall have an
account of the "function" of religion.

Philosophy, we have argued, is also a practical discipline,
and we may approach the solution of our problem by asking:
What can religion do which philosophy cannot? Why is not
philosophy alone adequate for the acquisition of virtue?
Let us admit, first of all, that philosophy can give us an
adequate definition or description of virtue, of what is good
or right. Does it follow from this that when we are armed
with such an account of virtue that we shall desire to attain
it? It clearly does not. One can have a theoretical intuition of
the nature of virtue without having either the power or desire to achieve it. The disparity between our knowledge of
our duties and our power to perform them is a major source
of all tragedy, and desire to achieve virtue, since it is essentially an attitude (an attitude of the will, according to the
older psychology), is not capable of being influenced by
definitions and descriptions addressed to our reason or power
of judgment. Philosophy must *presuppose* a practical interest
in the outcome of its researches; it cannot induce it. The

philosopher may have this interest, as all men have it to some degree, but philosophy will never intensify his moral concern. There are no philosophical arguments which demonstrate that one *ought* to be interested in virtue. Only religion can implant a desire for perfection or keep alive that modicum of interest which each of us possesses. This it can do because its methods are persuasive rather than argumentative, arational rather than rational, rhetorical rather than logical. When we wish to encourage an attitude or implant a disposition of the heart or will, then reason is helpless. Bertrand Russell has stated this fact in the form of a dilemma: "Only kindliness can save the world, and even if we knew how to produce kindliness we should not do so unless we were already kindly." [3] In so far as kindliness is an attitude or a disposition it can be induced only by religion.

Religion therefore is devoted to the attainment of self-perfection, or to the equivalent ideal which we may call "the remaking of human nature." In the words of THE DHAMMA-PADA: "Irrigators guide the water (wherever they like); fletchers bend the arrow; carpenters bend a log of wood; wise people fashion themselves." [4] It is not surprising then that religion should have affinities with applied sociology and psychology. Religion, however, is not a species of technology, relying on scientific knowledge and adopting certain physical means for the achievement of preconceived ends. Its ultimate ends are often not clearly defined, as philosophers are quick to point out, and rather than attempt to mold character by gradual changes in the physical organism or its environment, it prefers to induce by its own methods a quick and decisive change of character, that which is usually called a "conversion." It prefers to believe that if this disposition of the heart is not itself the ultimate perfec-

[3] *Icarus*, Dutton, 1924, p. 62.
[4] *The Dhammapada*, tr. by Irving Babbitt, Oxford, 1936, p. 14.

tion and happiness, it is the surest means of attaining that perfection, whatever it may prove to be.

With this characterization it is easy to see how religion proper differs from magic. A clear account of magic is given in the following quotation: "The fundamental aim of all magic is to impose the human will on nature, on man or on the supersensual world in order to master them. To speak the language of Schopenhauer, magic is used in the service of the Will and is therefore akin to applied science; whereas pure science and art are concerned with the disinterested contemplation or investigation of nature and life." [5] The intent of magic is to control natural or if possible supernatural forces for what Otto calls the "natural ends of man." [6] Magic is related therefore to genuine religion in much the same fashion that art is related to craft and science to technology. Magical acts are performed, not for the sake of any intrinsic value they may possess, but as means to the achievement of certain preconceived ends, and these ends may be of the most trivial or "natural" kind. Magic is distinguished from applied science or technology in that it makes no use of anything resembling scientific knowledge. The connection between the act as cause and the result to be effected is regarded as intrinsically mysterious and inexplicable. It differs from religion in that it makes no attempt at a direct transformation of the will itself but rather strives to achieve ends previously and arbitrarily determined by the will. When the propitiation of the supernatural or possession of the holy is regarded as valuable for its own sake, then and not until then does the true *vita religiosa* begin. [7] When this occurs, there is an immediate and ecstatic contemplation of the beauty of holiness and the characteristic humbling and exaltation of the will in worship.

[5] E. M. Butler, *Ritual Magic*, Cambridge, 1949, p. 3.
[6] Rudolph Otto, *op. cit.*, p. 33.
[7] *Ibid.*, p. 33.

2. *PARADOX*

To the historian of culture the recurrent attempts by theologians of all creeds to provide a rational foundation for religion must certainly appear the most curious example of human fatuity. To insist that religion *needs* a rational foundation, is to misinterpret its very nature, and to introduce rational principles into religion is to transform it into a kind of spurious metaphysics. Religious faith is an act of will accomplished in the face of that which is intrinsically unintelligible and mysterious and paradoxical. And this is no mere accidental property of religion. As Otto has said, it is characteristic of religion to insist that there is "an *intrinsic value* in the incomprehensible." [8] Religion, in short, is attracted by the unintelligible and mysterious, and if anything appears to be ultimately and irreducibly inexplicable, it exerts for that very reason an even greater fascination. This attitude, of course, is intolerable to science which is interested only in what is capable of being understood and is interested in mystery only that it may dispel it. There is no point at which science and religion are more antithetical.

It is a little surprising then when scientists and theologians attempt to show that science can be used to confirm the truths of religion. Such attempts are made by naïve and well-meaning individuals in every generation and suffer the inevitable neglect which they deserve. They are plausible only to those who identify a religion with its residual creeds and dogmas and who believe furthermore that such dogmas can be interpreted by the same rules which apply to the sentences of science and metaphysics. Aside then from the logical follies committed by such individuals, there is the further question: Do religious utterances intend to "state

[8] *Ibid.*, p. 83.

facts" in the same sense in which scientific statements and
philosophic statements are statements of fact?

Let us consider the following passage from the ŚVETĀŚVA-
TARA UPANISHAD: [9]

> *The Soul (Ātman), which pervades all things*
> *As butter is contained in cream,*
> *Which is rooted in self-knowledge and austerity —*
> *This is Brahma, the highest mystic doctrine (upaniṣad)!*
> *This is Brahma, the highest mystic doctrine!*

I do not profess to know by what criterion theologians distinguish dogma from poetic figures of speech, but let us assume
that this passage is not merely an extended simile. What does
this profound and moving statement invite us to believe?
Surely not what it literally *says;* otherwise the organic chemist would possess the clearest conception of the relation of the
cosmic Self and the whole. Such a statement is clearly not
intended to be a statement of fact at all. It might better be
described as a statement or description of an intuition and
simultaneously an expression of feeling. In particular the
statement is not intended to *explain* how the Soul is related
to the whole. This would assume that the author thought he
knew how butter was contained in cream. It is presumably
more accurate to say that he intended to assert: "The Soul is
contained in the whole in the same mysterious way in which
butter is contained in cream." What is expressed here, however, is an intuition and a feeling, and no translation can
ever be literally accurate.

We are face to face again with the fact that what truly
profound religion is concerned with is that which is "wholly
other" than what we are familiar with in our ordinary
existence. Sometimes this results in paradoxical expressions
that God is a void or that blessedness is a state of non-being.

---

[9] *The Thirteen Principal Upanishads*, tr. by R. E. Hume, Oxford, 1934, p. 397.

In such expressions "void" and "non-being" are not to be identified with "non-existence," but merely with the "wholly other." What is asserted is merely negative: that God's nature and Nirvana are completely different from anything we can grasp conceptually. But again, to quote Otto, "while exaggerating to the point of paradox this *negation* and contrast—the only means open to conceptual thought to apprehend the 'mysterium'—Mysticism at the same time retains the *positive quality* of the 'wholly other' as a very living factor in its over-brimming religious emotion." [10] Conceptually we have a negation, an incomprehensibility; but this is accompanied by the purest and strongest religious emotion.

All exegesis therefore which attempts to "explain" the dogmas or creeds of a religion has set itself an impossible task. All defenders of "the reasonableness of Christianity" and all creators of a synthesis of religion and metaphysics or religion and physics have ended by providing sceptics and believers alike with grounds for doubt and uncertainty, and have discredited that which they wished most earnestly to defend. No religious conversion has ever been effected by argument alone. As Kant observed, proof can merely "prepare the understanding for theological knowledge and give it a straight and natural direction" but it cannot by itself give us theological knowledge; "it cannot do the job alone." [11] It required a Kierkegaard to remind us that all the fundamental tenets of Christianity are irreducible paradoxes, that faith is always a leap and never a gradual, safe progression, that the "knight of faith" is he who is strong enough to embrace the absurd and act from a conviction, which, if not higher than reason, springs at least from a source which is other than reason.

[10] *Op. cit.*, p. 30.
[11] *Kritik der Reinen Vernunft*, B 665.

This contrast of religion and philosophy appears in a dramatic form in Nietzsche's BIRTH OF TRAGEDY as the contrast between the Dionysian and the Socratic. The madness of the Dionysian worshipper; his shuddering intuition of the unutterable horror of existence; his passionate desire to divest himself of his own identity in an orgiastic revel and merge his own being with that of his suffering deity — all this is wonderfully contrasted with the rational, optimistic, self-sufficing, dialectical Socrates. If the Dionysian must be thought of as a dancer, then Socrates is the prototype of the non-dancer. (Xenophon, it is true, relates a story that Socrates practiced dancing at home, but to anyone who knows something of Socrates, nothing can be more incongruous.) Yet this same Socrates, as we have seen, is also the representative *par excellence* of philosophy or, as Nietzsche would have it, of scientific knowledge (*Wissenschaft*). If Nietzsche's argument is sound that Socrates through Euripides destroyed Greek tragedy, it is precisely because he destroyed all that was Dionysian and religious in Greek tragedy. If art becomes mere propaganda or debate when it becomes dialectical, it is likewise true that religion becomes trivial and feeble when it is intellectualized by the theologian and philosopher. One is left with a discipline which is neither passionate nor critical, neither hot nor cold, and it deserves to die the death of Greek tragedy.

3. *COMMITMENT*

In the previous section we have discovered the perennial concern of religion with that which is "wholly other," with entities and states of existence which are completely different from those which we can grasp by our senses and imagination. It was for this reason that we previously characterized religion, in opposition to art and science, as a transcendental discipline. But we have also discovered that religious utterances are not statements of fact, that is, unlike science they make no assertion of empirical fact and unlike philosophy no assertion of "transcendental fact." In most instances they make no assertion at all, if by "assertion" we mean "a statement which springs from an act of judgment," and for this reason we previously declared that religion, unlike science and philosophy, was not a discipline involving judgment. We may express this by saying that religious utterances are religious, not by reason of the fact that they may be interpreted as ordinary categorical statements or assertions, since we have seen that when so interpreted they become simple paradoxes, but for some other reason. We must now attempt to discover what this reason is.

If we postpone for the moment any consideration of religious intuition or religious knowledge, we shall find nevertheless that what is characteristic of a religious utterance is that it is the expression of an attitude, of an active "set" or disposition of the will. In this respect religious utterances are equivalent to exclamations, although it must be observed that they are not mere expressions of feeling but rather revelations of decisions and resolutions. Religious existence, as Kierkegaard has told us, is always a decisive *act*, and religious utterances are always a record therefore of genuine commitments. The religious man, as Pascal knew, is like a gambler; he must *choose* how he will lay his bets. There is no place here for mere theoretical consideration of the alternatives. "I know that my Redeemer liveth" is a record of a decision made, of an inflexible and joyful resolution, and should not be confused with utterances of the same form which are the expression of rational judgments.

As logicians and students of language know, sentences which are expressions of attitudes have also an imperative force, that is, they tend to induce similar attitudes in those who overhear such an utterance. Religious attitudes are induced by contagion rather than by doctrinal teaching. Even the individual worshipper in moments of despair may have recourse to his own previous utterances and insights, and these often have the form of imperatives directed to himself. We can persuade ourselves that this imperative character is no accident by remembering that the immediate aim of religion is to implant or encourage a certain disposition of the will, a disposition towards holiness or perfection. Religious insights are treasured because they tend to produce directly or by contagion (when uttered) this inner transformation of character, and religion is the systematic pursuit of these insights and moments of commitment for the sake of the final "cleansing of the inward parts," to use Whitehead's phrase.[12]

We can now understand the presence of paradox in religious utterances. If a sentence is the record of a commitment or an implicit imperative, it can only lead to nonsense and paradox to interpret it as if it were a simple categorical statement, the expression of what we have called a "rational judgment." Its religious meaning, at least, is not to be discovered by such an analysis. If it is the end of science and philosophy, each in its own way, to discover that such-and-such is the case, then it is true that each of them aims at the formulation of a rational judgment, expressible in a categorical proposition. This cannot be true of religion, however, since as we have seen, religious meaning is not identical with what is usually called "descriptive meaning." The aim of religion is not to arrive at any conclusion that such and such is the case; it aims instead at a direct, immediate transformation of character. Religious utterances are simultaneously the record of transformations already effected and the means to future transformations. It is for this reason that we have

[12] A. N. Whitehead, *Religion in the Making,* Macmillan, 1926, p. 15.

asserted that religion is a discipline which does not involve judgment.

4. *RELIGIOUS KNOWLEDGE*

I N the previous section we have asserted that religious utterances are the records of religious insights and acts of commitment, and all that we attempted to show was that in so far as a religious utterance was an expression of an act of commitment or an incitement to such an act, it did not involve judgment. This qualification is necessary since it might well be insisted that religious insight is knowledge and all knowledge involves judgment.

We must recur to a distinction which we used in our discussion of art, Russell's distinction between knowledge of things and knowledge of truths. We argued there that there is such a thing as artistic knowledge, but that it is knowledge of things, that is, knowledge by acquaintance, and not knowledge of truths. For this reason it does not involve judgment. Now it is precisely this same *kind* of knowledge which is characteristic of religious insight. These two species of knowledge by acquaintance differ, however, in this: artistic knowledge is knowledge of the immediate, of a content presented in sensation or imagination; religious knowledge is acquaintance with the transcendental. In the case of aesthetic experience acquaintance with sensuous content produces all those transformations within us which we experience as aesthetic pleasure in the presence of beauty. In religious experience direct apprehension of "the holy" produces in us the attitudes of awe, worship, and dedication characteristic of religion. What is significant is that in each instance what is presented to us is a content or "thing" and not a relationship or set of relationships. Relationships can be discovered only by an act of judgment; content can be apprehended

immediately by sensation or imagination or transcendentally
by intuition and insight.

This distinction has been noted by students of religion.
Otto asks, "How can we, too, come to experience in him
[Christ] 'holiness made manifest'?" His answer is: "Obviously not through demonstration and proof, by applying
some conceptual rule. We cannot suggest any conceptual
criterion in the form: 'When the elements X and Y are
brought together, a revelation results.' It is just this impossi-
bility which makes us speak of 'divination,' 'intuitive apprehension.' The experience must come, not by demonstration,
but by pure *contemplation*, through the mind submitting
itself unreservedly to a pure 'impression' of the object." [13]
Just as aesthetic experience springs from a pure impression
of sensuous content (we have called it "pure aesthesis"), so
religious experience springs from a pure impression of
transcendental content. Following Otto let us call it "pure
contemplation."

What is significant is that in all cases of genuine religious
revelation it is always "something" that appears: either an
angel of the Lord or a glorified image of Christ or Dionysus
or Buddha or, in Wordsworth's case,

> . . . *something far more deeply interfused,*
> *Whose dwelling is the light of setting suns,*
> *And the round ocean and the living air,*
> *And the blue sky, and in the mind of man . . .*[14]

In all cases it is a "sense of something," of something which
we may call, following Otto, "the holy." Nor is the "holy"
perceptible to ordinary vision. It is always "far more deeply
interfused." It is not visible nature which is intuited, otherwise such an intuition would give rise to art. Nature is

[13] *Op. cit.,* p. 172.
[14] *Tintern Abbey,* ll. 95–99.

merely the "garment of God," to use Goethe's phrase. Like-wise it is always the "wholly other" in religious personalities which fascinates the worshipper. The religious genius, re-garded aesthetically, would be the proper subject of a novel or biography; regarded religiously he becomes an object of worship.

We now have an additional clue to what may be called the "ineffability" of religion. The religious mystic usually complains that he cannot express in language his mystic vision. The convert will assert that no one who has not experienced the grace of God can know what he means when he talks about it. This is true not merely of religion but of all knowledge by acquaintance. It is notoriously impossible to describe in words the actual sound of a musical composition or the literal appearance of a painting or the taste of straw-berries. Knowledge of things, that is, knowledge by acquaint-ance, cannot be conveyed in language; it can only be evoked, or more properly, re-evoked. (Knowledge of complexes of things can be said to be evoked but only if there is already acquaintance with the elements of such complexes.) For this additional reason the language of the religious will always appear paradoxical and vague. He must always presuppose that his auditor knows what he is talking about; if the audi-tor does not know it (by acquaintance), he will always find such discourse nonsensical.

We must insist therefore on the importance of religious knowledge in religion, but we must remember that it is a transcendental knowledge of things and not a knowledge of truths and therefore does not involve judgment. Insight and commitment are then the two components of religious experience, but how are they related? Does one give rise to the other or are they mutually independent? Aesthetic apprehension, we have asserted, produces in us a reaction we have called "aesthetic pleasure" and "aesthetic pain."

(There are, of course, intervening degrees between "pure" pleasure and "pure" pain.) It is for this reason that Santayana called beauty "objectified pleasure." There is also an invariable reaction produced in us by religious insight: that which we have previously called "commitment." Devotion (or its contrary, revulsion) is always the result of pure contemplation as pleasure (or pain) is the result of pure aesthesis. Religious apprehension, like aesthetic apprehension, does not always find what it seeks. If it does find it, there is commitment to what is found. If it does not find it, there is a corresponding revulsion of the will. Just as no one is aesthetically sensitive who cannot experience aesthetic pain, so no one is religiously sensitive who cannot feel religious revulsion. Corresponding to a commitment of self in the presence of the holy, there is a withholding of self in the presence of the unholy. This is the source of religious feeling concerning tabus and sin.

Insight therefore may give rise to commitment, but conversely commitment may give rise to insight. Just as he who is disposed to seek for beauty usually finds it, so he who is committed to a search for holiness is rewarded by moments of pure and ecstatic contemplation. Thus contemplation intensifies commitment and commitment contemplation. The relation between the two components of the religious experience is thus organic and defies any more exact description.

5. *THE RELIGIOUS A PRIORI*

PHILOSOPHICAL objects of thought we called "transcendental" because they were not immediately presented in sensation or imagination. They were called a priori because they did not arise from sensation or imagination. Philosophical knowledge for the same reason was called a priori. One must not confuse this position with any doctrine of "innate" ideas. All that we are asserting is that the mind itself is active in the act of judgment which accompanies all knowledge and without help from the senses creates (or identifies) certain objects of thought by its own agency. For this reason we have asserted that thought is the origin of all philosophical, that is, all a priori knowledge.

We have likewise asserted that the objects of religious knowledge are transcendental, "wholly other" than the objects presented to us by sense and imagination. If we now ask about the *origin* of this knowledge, we are asking, Is religious knowledge likewise a priori? Is there a religious as well as a philosophic a priori? The situation seems to be the same as in the case of philosophy: all our religious knowledge begins with experience, but it does not arise out of experience, where by "experience" we mean, of course, "sense experience." The content of religious intuition seems not to arise from experience. Experience is, in fact, only the occasion for such knowledge. If thought is the origin of philosophic knowledge, then pure contemplation is the origin of religious knowledge, and if thought is the origin of philosophic knowledge because the mind is active rather than passive in such knowledge, then contemplation is the origin of religious knowledge because in such moments the will is active rather than passive. Religious insight is *sought;* it does not merely happen.

Philosophic knowledge is discursive knowledge; it appears in the form of statements. The test for such knowledge is: *Must* we believe such statements? Are they really absolute presuppositions? Religious knowledge is transcendental knowledge by acquaintance, and, as we have seen, such knowledge may produce in us commitment or revulsion or any attitude intermediate between these two. The test for genuine or satisfactory religious knowledge therefore is this:

Does it produce in us complete and wholehearted commitment? If the validity of philosophic knowledge must be
tested by the reactions of the mind, the validity of religious
knowledge must be tested by the reactions of the will, and
just as the mind's reactions are not determined by sensation
or imagination, so the reactions of the will are not determined
by experience. We find here with respect to the will a religious a priori which is the exact analogue of the philosophic
a priori. There is in short a religious "hunger" which is not
implanted by experience and which is not satisfied by any of
the numerous objects of experience. It is this set of the will,
this passion for the holy and divine, which evaluates all
those transcendental contents which appear as candidates for
devotion and worship.

A man is not a philosopher, we have said, because he
utters "philosophical" statements. Philosophy is not the act
of asserting absolute presuppositions but of discovering them,
and it requires dialectical and critical powers lacking in the
non-philosopher. Likewise religion is not merely hungering
and thirsting after righteousness. Religion is the activity
of seeking and finding that which will assuage and satisfy
this hunger. The religious genius, to use James's happy
phrase, is he in whom this hunger and thirst are intensified
but who possesses also a vision of God or man or nature, or
God, man, and nature, which satisfies his own religious hunger and that of other men as well. It is not surprising that
such men should themselves be worshipped and adored.

Otto has argued that the holy ought to be regarded as an
a priori category. This would tend to link it too closely,
however, to the a priori concepts of philosophy. The holy,
it must be remembered, is known by acquaintance in religious knowledge. It is that which is discriminated and
evaluated by an act of will, not of judgment. For this reason
we must remember that if thought is the origin of the philo-

sophic a priori, will is the origin of the religious a priori. This prior *need* is the source of all genuine religious knowledge and all positive commitment.

6. *REAL OR IDEAL?*

AN emphasis on the a priori leads ordinarily to subjectivism. In philosophy this appears as the doctrine that all relations are the work of the mind, that all a priori concepts are imposed on a structureless datum. It would follow from this doctrine that all thinking which introduces such concepts is nothing but a creative falsification which ascribes characteristics to the world of "things in themselves" which they do not really possess. Let us consider Plato's example in the THEAETETUS. The senses, he tells us, can present us with the sensations, say, of touch and vision, but no single sense, nor all of them together, could compare the sensation peculiar to one individual sense with some other sensation. In particular a single sense could not be aware that a sensation of touch was *different* from a sensation of vision. Those who argue that all relations are the work of the mind would insist that the relation of "difference" which holds between these two sensations must be provided by the mind, since it appears only in the act of judgment and cannot be provided by any of the senses.

It is important to note that Plato's language does not support this position. He makes Theaetetus say: ". . . I think there is no special organ at all for these notions, as there are for those others; but it appears to me that the soul views by itself directly what all things have in common." [15] It is quite possible, in short, that the mind does not supply the relational tie but merely *identifies* it. The relation may still be regarded as a priori in the sense that it does not arise

[15] 185 D.

from experience, that is, from sensation. To paraphrase Kant's famous statement, although it may be true that awareness of relations begins only when thinking begins, it need not follow that such relations must be regarded as the mere products of thinking. It is *possible* (but of course not necessary) that the mind by thinking can simply identify that which the senses cannot. This would seem to be Plato's own intention since in the TIMAEUS he constructs cosmological models for the two dialectical concepts, the Same and the Different. The theory of Forms, as expounded by Socrates in the PHAEDO, makes the same assumption: that the existence of a priori knowledge is compatible with the belief that the objects of thought of which we have philosophic knowledge are not created by the act of thinking but merely identified or recognized.

The Kantian position therefore that relations are the work of the mind is not entailed by the view that there is such a thing as a priori knowledge, nor on the other hand does such a view entail Platonic realism. An argument that a priori knowledge exists is not simultaneously an account of its natural *origin*. We attempted to distinguish these issues in our discussion of the sociology of knowledge. Whether the conditions of a priori knowledge are subjective, societal, or merely physical can not be decided by an analysis of such knowledge itself, and by the very nature of the concepts involved no scientific confirmation or disconfirmation of any one of these interpretations is possible.

What we do find, however, is this: that philosophy does *claim* objectivity for its judgments, that is, it presupposes that what it is talking about are not mere subjective phantoms of its own creation, and this is true of such abstract concepts as being and becoming, sameness and difference. Philosophy seeks to penetrate the world it talks about rather than create it, whether it conceives this world as an Absolute Experience or as a complex of material atoms. This assumption of an objective status for the transcendental objects of thought with which it deals is therefore an absolute assumption which underlies all philosophizing. This assumption cannot itself be demonstrated within metaphysics nor refuted by any critique of metaphysics. It is amusing in this connection to note that Kant himself in his "refutation of metaphysics" assumes naturally, in defiance of all his explicit contentions, that the world of things in themselves (noumena) is causally connected with the world of phenomena. The metaphysician assumes, at the risk otherwise of losing his sanity, that there is something lying beyond his own experience to the intimate nature of which he proposes to penetrate by the characteristic methods of philosophic thinking. One cannot ask him to deduce within his system that assumption which makes his thinking itself possible.

The situation is similar in the case of the religious a priori. If the a priori as religious hunger is not implanted by experience nor satisfied by objects drawn from experience, if genuine religious knowledge generates and is generated by volitional commitment, it would *seem* to follow that the objects of religious knowledge have a purely ideal or subjective status and are created by the act of religious experience. Such a view of religion, however, would transform it into idolatry, since we should be asked to worship objects of our own making. The objects of religious knowledge, those transcendental entities known by acquaintance and before which our will humbles itself, are experienced as given to us or attained by us but not as created by us in the act of religious knowledge.

According to the subjectivist theory of the philosophical a priori all relations are the work of the mind; according to the subjectivist theory of the religious a priori all objects of religious knowledge are the work of the will. The process of manufacture of such objects might therefore be studied by the methods of empirical psychology. The conception of a religious a priori is compatible, however, with another dogma: that the objects of our religious knowledge do actually exist and that the religious a priori is simply a power which we possess that enables us to apprehend such objects, a power which operates independently of experience and is not derived from it. We may even assert without fear of contradiction that the God whom we know has implanted this power in us. All of these dogmas, including subjectivism, are compatible with the belief in a religious a priori because no one of them (nor its contradictory) is entailed by this belief. We may say, as in the case of philosophy: a description of the religious a priori is not simultaneously an account of its origin, and by reason of the fact that the objects of religious knowledge are transcendental, no *scientific* account of its origin is possible. Religious experience can be *described* by empirical psychology, but it can never be understood—nor discredited.

We may express our conclusion by saying that the objects of religious knowledge are always experienced as *given* to us and therefore as objectively real or existent. The question, Do the objects that you worship really exist? will always appear irrelevant to the worshipper. The question itself cannot be answered by science, since, as we have seen, science proper has no means of determining whether anything is real or existent. It can merely determine whether a given object is experienced, but in this case the object is transcendental and by definition cannot be immediately experienced. Nor can metaphysics determine whether a religious object exists, since metaphysics can at best provide a criterion of existence or relational knowledge concerning certain objects of thought, whereas religious knowledge is knowledge by acquaintance. To the worshipper who has *found* the object of his worship by contemplation, the assurance of the metaphysician that this object is real adds nothing to its value, nor does the hesitancy of the metaphysician concerning its reality detract from its value. The worshipper would be merely convinced that in this latter case the philosopher had not found what he was looking for.

Religious knowledge experiences its objects as *given* and therefore as objectively existent, and if it is not wholly indifferent to the theoretical question of their objective reality, and it usually is, it would seem to apply without critical forethought Plato's criterion of the real: [16] that to be real means to have the power of making a difference (or of being affected by something else). Since that which the worshipper knows in the act of pure contemplation has the effect of completely transforming his character and will, he is assured of its unquestionable reality—and simultaneously of his own.

[16] *Sophist*, 247 D–E.

[SEVEN]

Education

1. THE FUNDAMENTAL DISCIPLINES

". . . THE to-a-certain-degree mode of thought (that travesty on tolerance which mediates everything without petty scrupulosity), regarded as negative by the ancients, has now become positive; and what the ancients regarded as positive, the passion for distinctions, has now become a childish folly." [1] The foregoing chapters have been an attempt to rehabilitate this passion for distinctions. As long as we attempt to make one discipline do the work of another, as long as we are complacently ignorant of where one leaves off and another begins, as long as we believe that one shades off imperceptibly into another or attempt to reduce them all to one primitive discipline, so long will there be confusion and intolerance and frustration in our intellectual and cultural life. What is needed is a fixation of boundaries, and, although the preceding chapters are little more than a sketch of what is required, they may serve as a preliminary outline for a more detailed account.

One question in particular will need to be considered in such an account: Are there only four fundamental disciplines? Why, in particular, should we not include history, sociology, economics, psychology as disciplines coördinate

[1] S. Kierkegaard, *Philosophical Fragments*, tr. by D. F. Swenson, Princeton, 1936, p. 75.

139

with those we have called fundamental? The answer is not easy, and I can merely indicate briefly my grounds for rejecting their claim to be considered independent fundamental disciplines. The case of psychology is easily disposed of. Psychologists have quite recently become aware that what passed as psychology one hundred or even fifty years ago was principally a mixture of metaphysics and bad science. Psychology has learned, principally from behaviorism and operationalism, that what it can determine about human reactions and human nature must be determined by exactly the same methods which the physicist and chemist use in their laboratories. The "mind," in particular, as Carroll Pratt has pointed out,[2] is no longer an object of study in psychology. Human reactions must be studied in the same fashion that one studies all other physical events, and one leaves discussions of minds, selves, and egos to the metaphysician.

What shall we say of economics and sociology? Economists are not agreed concerning the proper method of economics, but this much at least is clear: that one major task of economics is to determine what the facts are, another to provide a theory for the "explanation" of these facts. In either respect, the methods of economics are no different from those of any other descriptive and statistical science, although there is the same tendency here to provide hypotheses as explanatory devices rather than simple generalizations. The descriptive method is still possible, however, and admittedly fruitful, and this, as we have seen, is the characteristic method of science. What shall we say, however, concerning discussions of value in economics? I cannot believe that there is any discussion of value in economics which cannot be handled by the methods of philosophy, provided it

[2] "The Meaning of Mind" in *Structure, Method and Meaning, Essays in Honor of Henry M. Sheffer*, Liberal Arts Press, 1951, pp. 209–16.

does not fall within the province of economic theory in the scientific sense mentioned above. Definitions of value, I should insist, are mere applications of more general definitions provided by philosophy. If this *is* the case, then the method of economics would be merely a complex of the methods of science and philosophy.

Somewhat the same remarks apply to sociology. The titular founder of sociology is also one of the founders of positivism, and it was Comte's aim to give a descriptive account of social phenomena which would be free from the metaphysical rubbish characteristic of the older theories. There is no doubt that the discovery of social laws, the exact analogue of physical laws, is one of the major tasks of sociology, and in this respect sociology belongs to science. But in so far as sociology is concerned with what *ought* to be done, in so far as it is "social philosophy," I should argue that it belongs properly to philosophy and that it is merely applying to social groups criteria of what is good and right which it discovers by the methods of philosophy. Thus sociology is also a complex of science and philosophy.

The case of history is more difficult. It is an older discipline than sociology or economics. In Greek culture it is coeval with science and philosophy. Why should we not regard it as a fifth fundamental discipline? If it were agreed, as often occurs in such discussions, that history is the record of particular facts while science is concerned only with general laws, then history would certainly be a fifth discipline, but is this assumption correct? If I have determined that the melting point of this particular bit of silver is such and such, am I a historian or a physicist? It is true that much of what we should now call zoölogy and ecology was once called "natural history," but *historia* originally was a general term which meant roughly "research" (or the results of "research"). This illustration in fact shows that what was previously called "history" has now been recognized to be nothing but science. Science, we have argued, is simply the attempt to discover that which is the case, and although the scientist is not completely happy until he has arrived at some general law, his result is no less scientific for being particular rather than general. The answer to such a question as "Did Socrates drink the hemlock in 399 B.C.?" must be provided, therefore, by the ordinary methods of scientific hypothesis and confirmation.

There is an imaginative or creative element in history, however, which does not appear in science. The historian is not content merely to marshal his facts and hypotheses; he orders them and embellishes them. He is interested, not merely in what the facts were, but in the facts themselves, and this intrinsic interest in fact is indistinguishable from an aesthetic interest. This is the aspect of history which is accentuated in the historical novel and the literary biography. It is for this reason that history is classified in certain university curricula as lying both within the field of the humanities and that of the social sciences. The historian is a literary creator (and not merely by reasons of style) as well as a custodian of scientific facts. Once the modern conception of science is introduced, the method of history is seen to be a complex of the methods of science and art.

2. EDUCATION AND METHODOLOGY

WE must now consider what use can be made of such abstract methodological results. In a paper which is little more than a *précis* of the argument of this book,[3] I have suggested that objective methodology has been carried on in the past principally by educational administrators and theorists. They

[3] "The Method of Methodology" in *Structure, Method and Meaning, Essays in Honor of Henry M. Sheffer*, Liberal Arts Press, 1951, pp. 152–70.

have used it as a means of answering the question, "What is each discipline good for?" One cannot give an account of the instrumental value of a discipline without having some conception of the nature of the discipline, and to know what a discipline is, is to know the method which characterizes that discipline. What is significant is that the educator has no axe to grind; he is not a polemic methodologist. He is not concerned to show that one of them is better than another but to assess the contributions of each to his own chosen ends.

But if it is true that only educators have been objective methodologists, it is not true that all educators have been. The reason is simply this: if the educator in assessing the educational value of a given discipline takes the account of that discipline from the practitioners of the discipline, he obtains ordinarily a set of conflicting *claims* and no coherent or intelligible account of how these disciplines are related to each other. He must *construct* a coherent account of these disciplines for himself, and most educators have refused to undertake the task.

Fortunately there are two great geniuses of Western culture who have dedicated their efforts to the solution of this problem: Plato and Kant. If the aim of education is simply human perfection or human culture (in the literal sense), then such a work as the REPUBLIC must be considered a magnificent treatise on education. We have here not merely a study of the political conditions for human perfection but an account of the contributions of music, poetry, art, science, religion, and philosophy to the attainment of such perfection. Philosophy itself is viewed as a means to the education of the philosopher-kings and not as an end in itself. As for Plato himself, how can one call the author of the SYMPOSIUM and the PHAEDO, the director of the first great scientific institute, the teacher of practical administrators and lawyers merely a philosopher? The proper title for Plato is that of educator, as a man passionately devoted to the acquisition of human virtue, the final articulate protagonist and representative of that ideal of harmonious and rounded development for which we must still use the Greek word *paideia*.

Plato's codification of the ideals of Greek *paideia* became the foundation of the later conception of "liberal education," and until the nineteenth century the aims of formal liberal education were almost identical with Plato's. But about a hundred years ago educators became aware that only lip-service was being paid to such ideals and that what ordinarily passed as such was neither liberal nor "useful." The demand, however, was not for a return to the older ideal but for a total abolition of the caricature. Only in Nietzsche do I find any defense of the older Greek conception: "The philosopher, as *we* free spirits understand him — as the man of the greatest responsibility, who has the conscience for the general development of mankind — will use religion for his disciplining and educating work, just as he will use the contemporary political and economic conditions." [4] Here, it must be noted, religion is to be *used*, and it is to be used for the general development of mankind. The notion that religion should be used would ordinarily appear as anathema both in those circles in which it is despised and in those in which it is venerated. Nietzsche is also aware that by "philosopher" he means something quite different from a *Privatdozent*. He means, it is clear, an educator.

Kant, unlike Plato, did not possess the advantage of a native familiarity with the Greek ideals. Religion, and a rather narrowly circumscribed religion, provided the initial impetus for his search, and without the intellectual stimulus of his efforts to temper the conflict of science and religion, of reason and faith, his results would have been trivial. One is tempted to say that Kant merely deduced the educational

[4] *Beyond Good and Evil*, chap. III, §61.

consequences of his discoveries in objective methodology, but it is equally possible that a religious concern for human perfection and the possibilities of its attainment motivated his researches in methodology. The consequence is, at any rate, that he reaches a position almost identical with that of Plato and Nietzsche: "The mathematician, the natural scientist, the logician are only craftsmen in the use of reason (*Vernunftkünstler*), however excellent the achievements of the first two in rational knowledge and the achievements of the second two in philosophical. There is also an ideal teacher (*Lehrer im Ideal*), who applies all these and uses them as tools in order to further the actual ends of human reason. He alone must we call the philosopher." [5] Here science and the scientist, rather than religion, are to be used to advance the ends of human nature, but Kant, like Nietzsche, insists that this ideal teacher be called a philosopher. No discovery or analysis of the laws of human reason, however, if this *be* the end of philosophy, will provide an account of how such laws or such acts of discovery are to be used nor of the relation of philosophy itself to science and religion. The "ideal teacher" is simply an educator who makes use of objective methodology for his own ends. This is certainly the achievement of Kant, regardless of his proposed nomenclature, that he has attempted to show us in impressive detail the interrelations of science, philosophy, art, and religion. Kant, like Plato, was not merely a philosopher in the strict sense; he also had acknowledged scientific gifts and a natural propensity toward religion. He lacked aesthetic sensibility and, as every reader knows, the gift of clear literary expression, but he seems to have possessed at any rate a sound knowledge of classical literature. In the case of these two educators, as they should properly be called, Whitehead's statement does not apply that "the task of coördination is left to those who

[5] *Kritik der Reinen Vernunft*, B 867.

lack either the force or the character to succeed in some definite career." [6]

3. *EDUCATION AND TRAINING*

THERE is a discipline therefore, distinct from the fundamental disciplines and from methodology, which is concerned with the use of the fundamental disciplines and which in turn uses the results of objective methodology. This discipline we have called education, and we have listed two distinguished representatives of this discipline. We must now attempt to justify our use of the word "education" in this sense.

It will be objected on the one hand that to say, as we have said, that the aim of education is simply human perfection or human culture is to say too much. According to this "definition" the doctor who sets our bones would be an educator. Nor is the eugenicist who wishes to improve the overall quality of the human strain ordinarily called an educator. It will also be objected that our definition is too narrow: to be educated is to be taught, to be taught is to be instructed, to be instructed is to be trained, and to be trained is to be trained *within* one discipline or some subdivision of it. Thus all questions concerning the use of a given discipline would reduce to questions concerning the social use of the practitioners of such a discipline and would belong properly to political theory. This is actually the way the question is being formulated now with regard to science: How best can the scientist be used in an industrial and increasingly militaristic society?

The first objection is a valid one; we were too careless in defining the characteristic aim of education. To aim at the improvement of human nature does not make one an educa-

[6] *Science and the Modern World*, Macmillan, 1925, p. 283.

tor; one might be in fact merely a political reformer. Education is not the act of improving human nature; it is the act of providing individuals with the means whereby they may accomplish their own improvement. Thus if I provide my generation with a new political philosophy, I am an educator; if I alter directly the political or social structure of my group, I am a social reformer. It is in this sense that one must understand the statement that all education is self-education. Literally this is nonsense; self-education is a contradiction in terms. What the individual does is to learn how to perfect himself by the use of means which have been externally provided.

It is now possible with this amendment to understand why there should be different types of education. If the self is identified with the physical body, then education is coterminous with physical education. If we wish to perfect the religious self, then we use religious education. If we conceive of the individual merely as a potential craftsman, then education becomes merely technical education. The question immediately arises: Are not these "selves" to which these special types of education are addressed merely aspects of human nature and is not there some discipline which should be concerned with the coördination and evaluation of these special types of education? This discipline is exactly that which I have previously called "education," and our previous definition must be amended to read: Education is concerned with the provision and evaluation of the means by which human individuals can perfect themselves as individuals.

The second objection, which depends on the argument that education is training within a given discipline, rests on a serious confusion between education and training. If teaching be considered as the act of training, then teaching is a craft, with all the characteristics we previously identified.

There is a specific, preconceived end, that the individual should be able to perform certain operations, solve certain problems, or know certain facts, and the act of training is done for the sake of this end. This is the view of teaching held by most university faculties and in particular by schools of education. It assumes that teaching is a technique and that if one masters this technique, which of course can itself be taught, then one is automatically a good teacher. There is this much truth in the theory: that if one is interested in producing a technologist, then one does it by training. The craftsman is produced by training, but it does not follow that the artist or scientist can be produced in the same way. If it were true, then our own country with its gigantic educational apparatus ought to be turning out each year hundreds of scientists alone. The fact is that the United States in the past century and a half has produced thousands of competent technicians and only a handful of creative scientists, and these have been principally pure mathematicians and theoretical physicists, since these by the very nature of their interests are least tempted to become technical consultants and inventors. Pure science died in the ancient world when the Greeks began making gadgets, and one can foresee a somewhat similar end to science in our contemporary Western world if the present trend toward technology continues.

If training produces merely the craftsman and technologist and not the artist and scientist, it is equally true that it does not produce the philosopher and the religious. Religious training can teach merely the dogmas and observances of a religion; it can *make* no one religious. Both Plato and Kant insisted that philosophy could not be taught at all. In one of his letters Plato says of his own doctrine: "There does not exist, nor will there ever exist, any treatise of mine dealing therewith. For it does not at all admit of verbal expression like other studies, but, as a result of continued application to the subject itself and communion therewith, it is brought to birth in the soul on a sudden, as light that is kindled by a leaping spark, and thereafter it nourishes itself. . . . And if I had thought that these subjects ought to be fully stated in writing or in speech to the public, what nobler action could I have performed in my life than that of writing what is of great benefit to mankind and bringing forth to the light for all men the nature of reality? But were I to undertake this task it would not, as I think, prove a good thing for men, save for some few who are able to discover the truth themselves with but little instruction; for as to the rest, some it would most unseasonably fill with a mistaken contempt, and others with an overweening and empty aspiration, as though they had learnt some sublime mysteries." [7] One cannot conclude from this that philosophers are born and not made, but merely that instruction is not sufficient to make one a philosopher and that where it is effective, very little of it is required. Admittedly it is necessary, but it merely provides the means by which an individual makes himself a philosopher.

4. CONCENTRATION

THE educational theorist who insists that education is simply training within a given discipline may reluctantly admit that such training ordinarily produces only the craftsman, the technologist, the dialectician, and the ritualist and not the artist, scientist, philosopher, or religious, but he will fervently insist that education is still concentration, that is, it is education within a single discipline. He will argue that the individual who has not learned to do something well and has not devoted himself, heart and soul, to his

[7] *Seventh Letter*, 341 C–E.

chosen field, has not been educated. We have here a genuine problem which is not easily resolved.

We must attempt to clarify this problem by noting that there are certain issues with which we are not concerned. We are not asking, for example, whether concentration within a particular field is apt to make one a more successful practitioner *in* that field. Ordinarily, if one wishes to be a competent scientist, one must confine one's attention to science, to the exclusion of everything else, through a good many hours of one's existence, and the same holds true for art, philosophy, and religion. The old saying is: *omne determinatio est negatio,* all determination (definiteness) is a negation, and no one attains any depth of experience in any one discipline without excluding everything else from his attention. Even here, however, there are instances in which a knowledge of philosophy has been helpful to the scientist or theologian and a knowledge of science to the philosopher and artist. We are not attempting to answer this question, however, but a more fundamental one: Should we call a man educated who has a competency, however great, in merely one discipline? Is human perfection possible only at the price of specialization and concentration? Is a great artist or a great scientist or a great philosopher a great man?

The answer is difficult, precisely because it presupposes that we know what we mean by "a great man," that is, by "human perfection." The answer must be supplied by philosophy, and on this point Greek philosophy at least was unequivocal. Human perfection could be attained only by the exercise of all those cultural capacities which are recognized as distinctively human, those roughly which we have called the four fundamental disciplines. Plato praises the philosopher's life above all others, it is true, but the ideal philosopher must have a thorough grounding in music (music and poetry in our sense) and religion, and he must have studied pure science for ten years, long enough to make him a competent scientist. Burnet points out [8] that Aristotle's description of *theoria*, the highest virtue, is intended to include aesthetic and artistic contemplation as well as purely scientific and philosophic contemplation, and it is clearly intended to include religious contemplation as well. Nor are these merely the precepts of Plato and Aristotle; they represent their practice as well.

I should like to suggest that this passion for wholeness is logically related to the passion for distinctions which Kierkegaard observed to be characteristic of the "ancients." Plato with all his love of mathematics makes Socrates and Glaucon agree in the REPUBLIC [9] that very few mathematicians are dialecticians or "good reasoners." What he means clearly is that very few mathematicians can think well about anything except mathematics. The realm of mathematics must be transcended in order to reach that of dialectic, but it is nevertheless a necessary propaedeutic to dialectic. Each discipline has its own function; none is adequate alone but none can be neglected. What is implied in Plato's account of art, for example, is that to be an artist unfits one for being a philosopher. This follows also from the distinctions we have drawn in the preceding chapters. The paradox is, however, that although these disciplines are antithetical, both are necessary for a complete life. What Plato is describing is the ideal of a flexible mind, unwarped by professionalism and specialization, taught to abstract from each discipline that peculiar contribution which it makes to human perfection.

It must also be observed that this was the ideal of the great creative epochs in Greek science and philosophy, the sixth and fifth centuries B.C., as well as the ideal of the fourth,

[8] John Burnet, *Aristotle on Education*, Cambridge, 1936, p. 8.
[9] 531 D–E.

and it persisted until the rise of professionalism in the Alexandrian culture. It reappeared again briefly in the Renaissance and seems to have disappeared entirely with Goethe. What is left is an ideal of professionalism and an educational system which produces automatons who learn their science from the Sunday supplement and their political philosophy from the illustrated weeklies. What is peculiarly tragic in this situation is that such a system does not produce super-automatons to control and direct the technical activities of the scientist, artist, and philosopher, perhaps for the simple reason that if there were anyone capable of doing this, he would not be an automaton.

5. FORMAL AND INFORMAL EDUCATION

WE have defined the end of education as the provision and evaluation of the means by which human individuals can acquire perfection for themselves as individuals, more shortly, as the provision and evaluation of the means to self-perfection. According to this definition, a father who buys a set of blocks for his child or teaches him to whistle is educating him, and I should not wish to deny this. Such education, however, we ought to call "informal" and reserve the word "formal" for education accomplished by institutions created especially for that purpose or by individuals who consider teaching a primary responsibility. The distinction is not always easy to make, since one could be formally educated, for instance, by one's father. The distinction must be made, however, to indicate that there are certain agencies — the family, the church, the club, the theatre, the press, the radio — which are not usually classified as educational and which yet provide for many individuals the only education, other than technical, which they possess. We need to consider therefore the relative importance of these two types of education and the relations which hold between them.

Even a brief survey of the formal education given by our schools, colleges, and universities reveals that most of it is either scientific or technological, in the sense in which we have defined these terms. Children are taught skills — how to print, how to write, how to read, how to do (blindly) certain arithmetical operations — and they are taught facts about the past, about the earth on which they live, about physical nature. There is no formal instruction in dancing; once a week the children sing together in the presence of the singing teacher. Once or twice a week the drawing teacher appears; otherwise the children are encouraged to "express themselves." Except in parochial schools, any genuine religious education is completely lacking. We have here, oddly enough, the paradox that the secular character of our formal education is due principally to religious bigotry.

Nor is the emphasis essentially different in "higher" education. Most of the courses offered in our universities and colleges are scientific or technological, in the sense in which we have been using these terms, and even here there is an increasing emphasis on technology at the expense of genuine science. Nor is this emphasis confined to the faculties of science; the humanities also are dominated by the methods of technology and its elaborate techniques. In the literature faculties one is taught the skills of reading and speaking and writing the language, one is taught the historical facts concerning a language and its literature, but does one ever receive an impetus which encourages one to *create* anything in that language like the works of art so meticulously studied? I do not wish to deride literary scholarship; some forms of it are among the purest instances of scientific activity that we possess. I am deploring merely that nothing else seems to be taught in our literature faculties. The instruction in philosophy is no healthier. History of philosophy and logic must be taught as necessary equipment for the philosopher, but logic is a science, and history of philosophy, if it is genuine scholarship and not merely a set of glib, imaginative generalizations, is itself science, since it is attempting to say as accurately as possible what so-and-so said and believed. But any amount of history of philosophy and logic will not by itself lead a student to do philosophy. As in the case of literature, his training has not enabled him to create the sort of thing which he himself reads so carefully. The student of history is encouraged to read history and remember it, but is he encouraged to *write* it? The situation is even worse in the case of religion. In a great many institutions of higher learning religion is not taught at all, or if it is taught, the teaching is not intended to make anyone religious. Instruction in applied art is almost wholly lacking. We have the anomaly that one can "receive credit" for a course in the history of art or in counterpoint but no credit, or very little, for *doing* art or music. All such activities, including drama and dancing, are extracurricular, organized by the students themselves, if they are organized at all. The situation is improving, particularly in some of the progressive colleges, but it is still deplorable. And lastly one might mention the caricature which passes as physical education. Departments of physical education have become departments of athletics, and the difference is enormous.

If our formal education is principally scientific, technical, and professional, then any education we receive in the other disciplines must be obtained informally. I do not wish to deny the effectiveness of informal education. The danger is that such education will not be done at all or that it will be done badly. (Education, like art and science, can be bad as well as good.) The result is, when such a cultural hiatus exists, that it is bound to be exploited by the "mass media." When one surveys the overall character of the press, movies, radio, and television in our own country, it is difficult to resist the feeling that never before in the history of Western culture has a population of one hundred and fifty million individuals been so completely and systematically vulgarized. What is particularly tragic is that such vulgarization results, not merely from the self-interest of these agencies themselves, but from the fact that the public is getting "what it wants." By means of the irresponsible policy which attempts to provide an uneducated public with what it wants, rather than with what it needs, cultural depravity perpetuates itself, and we have a social situation very little different from that which produced the "bread and circuses" of the decadent Roman empire.

It is perhaps only natural that the commercial mass media (or the advertising agencies which control them) should refuse to accept any educational responsibilities and should prefer rather to exploit the education [10] or the lack of it on the part of their audience. It is a little more surprising when educational administrators and governing boards wish to renounce this responsibility and even attempt to formulate their grounds for such a rejection as an educational philosophy. The first step in this direction was the introduction of the elective system at Harvard. The net result of this innovation, it is now seen very clearly, was to ask the uneducated student to formulate for himself a program and philosophy of education. I should like to deny, if it is necessary to do so, that the average student is in a position to do this. It is difficult to believe that mere lack of experience qualifies one for such an important responsibility, and a glance at the jumble of courses presented by most candidates for graduation will vividly confirm this suspicion.

According to the elective theory the student determines

[10] One must remember that a newspaper, for example, can miseducate its readers only because they are literate.

merely what courses he will take. There is another popular theory, however, which goes even further. This theory, that of "progressive education," would also insist that the student determine how each course is to be taught. According to this theory subject matter is unimportant, provided it interests the student, and one is entitled to begin with anything — turkeys, the dance, or the student's interest in himself. The educator dare not attempt to implant new interests; he must begin with those the student already has, no matter how fortuitously they may have been acquired. Interest is sacred; imposition, and therefore tradition, are suspect. The course must be altered to fit the student, not the student to fit the course.

It must be admitted that progressive education is preferable in many respects to the caricature of liberal or traditional education which it supplanted. It may also be admitted that in the nursery school one *must* begin with interests which the child already possesses (although even here certain character traits must be imposed and cannot be merely elicited). It does not follow that one should apply such methods to anyone who is not a baby. This would presuppose, first of all, that the child or adolescent has the *right* interests and secondly that he can be trusted to determine the methods by which those interests may be satisfied. But children are not angels nor are they all geniuses, and the net result of this philosophy and this program is simply protracted infantilism in its products. If it was a characteristic vice of the older education to make little men and women out of children, it is characteristic of the new to produce men and women who are nothing but children. Progressive education beyond the nursery level is an indulgence and a subtle way of flattering the student, and only the well-to-do can provide it for their children. There are indications, however, that even the indigent classes of our society are yearning for this "prolongation of infancy." [11] One can hardly explain otherwise the pleasure which a growing number of adults receive from the comic strip and the equally childish entertainment provided by the movies and radio. The "myth of the child," established by Rousseau and buttressed by the "scientific" findings of child psychology, may well prove to be the characteristic myth of our generation.

6. THE POSITIVE IDEAL

I f "to educate" means "to provide *and* evaluate the means of self-perfection," then it is clear that the proponents of the elective theory and of progressive education have refused to accept their full educational responsibility. The student in most cases cannot and will not attempt such an evaluation. The result is that the educator merely evaluates the means of attaining a good technical education and leaves to the student the task of evaluating the means to his education as a human being. In this task he receives little help from the "informal" agencies, since they, by definition, are more interested in furthering their own interests, commercial or sectarian, than in education as such. The result is that no one, except an occasional troubled educator, feels any sense of educational responsibility in the complete sense, unless it be the unhappy and unfortunate student. Such a situation is intolerable, and what is required is the formulation of some sort of educational ideal, some evaluation of the means which may be employed in the achievement of human perfection, and some account of the relations which hold between these means.

For this purpose, I have argued, objective methodology is indispensable. Before we can decide how religion or science or technology should be used, we must decide what they are,

[11] "We cannot recur too often in educational matters to the conception of John Fiske, that advance in civilization is an accompaniment of the prolongation of infancy." John Dewey in *Education Today*, ed. by J. Ratner, 1940, p. 25.

but this knowledge of what they are provides fortunately an immediate clue to how they ought to be used. Our fundamental assumption is that every cultural discipline must be regarded as a means and not as a possible end in itself. Virtue is not to be found within any one discipline but only in a proper blending of them all, nor is any one of our fundamental disciplines to be considered less of a means than technical training which is admittedly instrumental.

If we rely on our previous accounts of the nature of each of our fundamental disciplines, we can construct a brief outline of the educational function of each. If human perfection is to be measured by the quality of human experience and of those dispositions of character which tend to eventuate in certain types of experience, and I find this a plausible assumption, then it is the function of art to provide us with a certain quality of sensuous and imaginative experience, that which comes from the creation and apprehension of beautiful things and movements and which we usually call "aesthetic pleasure." It is the function of science to provide us with a certain sort of experience which comes from the apprehension of explicit relationships within the manifold presented by sense and imagination. The characteristic mark of such experience is the "pleasure of discovery" which accompanies and suffuses it, something we might call "scientific pleasure." Such types of experience are instances or components of human perfection but they are not *concerned* with human perfection. They ordinarily appear fortuitously therefore. Religion *is* concerned with the attainment of human perfection and in particular with implanting or intensifying a love of what is good or holy or perfect. It is the function of religion, in short, to make us desire perfection by producing a certain disposition of character or will toward that which is transcendentally perfect and holy. But religion may have, and often does have, depraved or vague conceptions of human perfection and of its metaphysical conditions and foundations. It is the function of philosophy, by its methods of analysis and intuition, to clarify and refine such conceptions and indicate explicitly their relevance to the attainment of virtue.

These components of an ideal human experience, however, cannot exist simultaneously, since by reason of the oppositions within our disciplines one cannot do philosophy and art at the same time nor science and religion. Nor can we insist that a day's work should include them all. The proper temporal unit for judging human experience, as Aristotle knew, is a lifetime. Our conclusion must be expressed then in this fashion: that if a man has been *merely* an artist in his lifetime, he has not attained to human perfection, and the same may be said of each of the other disciplines. This becomes rather more plausible if we accept Aristotle's view that human virtue is the exercise of those capacities we possess which are peculiarly and distinctively human. Since, as we have argued, the capacity to do each of our fundamental disciplines is a distinctively human capacity, one cannot be a "complete man" without exercising this capacity. The mere scientist, the mere philosopher, the mere artist is then not completely human, nor is he human who exercises two or three of these capacities and spurns or neglects the others. Virtue is a harmony of cultural experience and activity, and disproportion or defect can produce merely discord and ugliness.

The usual objections to such a program are first, that it is impossible or impracticable and second, that it tends to emphasize extensity of experience rather than intensity or depth and therefore easily degenerates into dilettantism. Now it is necessary to insist that within each discipline there must be a genuine intensity of experience. One must not merely read science; one must *do* it. One must not merely enjoy art; one must be an artist. What is ordinarily forgotten is that the intensity of experience of the amateur artist is of exactly the same *kind* as that of his accomplished colleague, although the two products may be quite disproportionate. The child who discovers that every other number is even or the student beginning his study of the calculus can experience the same kind of pleasure as the accomplished mathematician. One is not a scientist by virtue of the fact that one is familiar with many sciences or even that one is a genius within one's own narrow field. Subject matter, in fact, is unimportant here. What is important is that one uses the *methods* of science. The educational consequences are that we ought to give each student not a wide range of scientific information, but an actual capacity to do science, even on an elementary level. The result may be that he can do only one science, but he will have a better knowledge of what science is than if he had read all the encyclopedias and handbooks. Only this sort of intensive experience in any discipline is worth its salt. It might be added that this kind of educational emphasis will permit the really gifted student to exercise his capacities to the full on subject matter which is no longer elementary.

Our formal education, if it is to fulfill this ideal, should not merely tell our students about religion or religions; it should make them religious. It should not merely portray the range of philosophical positions, historical and theoretical; it should encourage them to *take* a position. It should not merely acquaint them with art products and the history of art; it should make them into artists. It should not merely provide them with scientific information or technological training; it should make them learn to do science. Only in this way will our educational products be anything other than automatons and cultural monstrosities.

This extended answer to the second objection is also an

answer to the first. Such an educational ideal as we have
sketched is not impossible of attainment or impracticable if
we do not confuse intensity of experience in any one discipline
with range of information or complexity of subject matter.
What is important is that one learn to do science creatively,
even if the products of one's activity are less imposing than
those of a polished technician or a genuinely gifted neighbor,
and I should think that the ability to do some one science
could be taught somehow between the ages of six and twenty-
one. I should think also that in this period of fifteen years
each student could be taught to do one of the arts, if it were
only singing or speech. Nor do I believe that this period is
too short to give students a knowledge (by acquaintance) of
the meaning of religious experience, nor of the excitement
and satisfaction which come from thinking through for one's
self some of the fundamental problems in ethics and metaphysics. It is our existing education which emphasizes
extensity by its insistence on survey courses and range of
information. What is required is intensive experience within
the range of the four fundamental disciplines we have studied
in this book.

It might also be objected that such an educational ideal
is impossible because it does not provide for any sort of
technical or professional training, and for the increasing
number of individuals who must have such a training in order to exist at all in our society, such an education in the
fundamental disciplines would be a luxury which they could
not afford. It is quite true that the program we have sketched
would not attempt to train anyone to be a craftsman or
technician. It would attempt, however, to give every edu-
cable individual a minimum grounding in those cultural
disciplines with which he must have some acquaintance if he
is to enjoy a happiness which is genuinely human and not
merely animal or childish. (I shall allow the social theorist

to decide what to do with the increasing number of non-educable members of our society.) This minimum education should at least be available to all children in our society. If continued until maturity, it would tend to produce, not technicians and craftsmen, but genuine scientists, artists, philosophers, and "men of religion." I am assuming further-more that this alternative would be preferable to the present situation in which thousands of mere technicians and special-ists are turned out each year by our educational factories. I am not denying that technical training is necessary or valu-able; I am merely insisting that our fundamental education should be non-technical. It must be a genuine education in our fundamental disciplines rather than a training in their technical counterparts.

Technical training must be provided, but it should grow naturally out of an education in some fundamental discipline and not conversely. An education in biology can be excellent equipment for the student of medicine or surgery and a knowledge of sociology for the politician and social worker, but the converse does not hold in either case. Since technol-ogy always makes use of scientific knowledge for its own ends, a knowledge of science in fact is necessary for the technologist. I am arguing simply that one ought to get this scientific knowledge first for its own sake. If it is acquired later for the sake of its applications, one is no longer doing science.

Some sort of screening apparatus will probably be nec-essary. Since it is easier to train individuals than to educate them, technical high schools and institutes will have to be provided for those students who either cannot be educated or who do not wish to be. We should frankly admit, however, that such individuals are being merely trained, and the in-formal educational agencies which operate upon them and provide them with such cultural education as they receive should then be carefully scrutinized and controlled. All students who can be *educated* should have the opportunity of higher education in a college or university, by the aid of Federal scholarships and grants, if necessary. Those who cannot should be encouraged to begin their technical training in a scientific institute or art school or seminary. There is no point in trying to mix education and training as is now done in the majority of colleges and universities. The result is usually *neither* education nor training. The present trend, principally by reason of pressure from industry, is to convert the university into a training school for apprentices and future employees. If this effort succeeds, it will be the end of higher education in the strict sense. Colleges and universities must be provided finally for those students who can be educated above the secondary level. Such students may very well concentrate in one discipline more than in another, but the emphasis will still be on wholeness, on creativity rather than on technical polish. Again at the end of this period all those individuals who have genuine ability in some one discipline should be encouraged to pursue it in a professional graduate school, which ideally would not be merely a technical institute. Those who now seek technical training in law or medicine or business will at least have some cultural foundation which, if not specifically helpful in their technical studies, will at least provide them with the means of perfecting *themselves*, and this, we have argued, is all that one can ask of an education.

What has been presented in this section is not intended to be a detailed account of the manner in which our educational ideal is to be implemented. It is enough perhaps for the time being to sketch this ideal as clearly as possible and demonstrate its natural dependence on the results of objective methodology.